Faithful Navigators

Islamic Guidance for Confidently Raising Teenagers with Faith and Wisdom in a Digital World

—•———————❖———————•—

SARAH GULFRAZ

Dedication

~ Bismillah ~

May Allah (swt) accept our efforts and grant us success in this life and the next. Ameen.

In dedication to my loving family and all their support.

Contents

Chapter One

Introduction

F or parents, the adolescent years present some of the most challenging obstacles. Teens may believe that no one, especially their parents, can relate to them since they are navigating hormonal changes and an increasingly complicated environment. As a result, the adolescent may experience complex challenges and feel confused, angry, and alone.

The digital age has caused our children to learn, interact, and see the world very differently. Information and entertainment are always at our fingertips because of the proliferation of smartphones, tablets, and the Internet. Although this exceptional degree of knowledge might inspire, it also poses several difficulties for Islamic parents.

Teens in the modern digital age are impacted by a greater number of digital components, including social media platforms, which frequently cause them to lose their creativity, time, and character. This book explores the complex dynamics of Islamic parenting in the digital age, highlighting the difficulties that this creates and arguing that Islamic educational ideas can be applied as a solid framework for solutions.

This book explores the deep lessons of Islam. It provides Muslim parents with helpful advice and insights to assist them in traversing the wonderful but difficult path of raising morally upright and well-balanced teens.

It is a priceless tool for contemporary Muslim parents who want to impart Islamic morals, ethics, and values to their children. Drawing from the traditions of Prophet Muhammad (PBUH) and the rich teachings of the Quran, it is an ardent and heartfelt examination of Islamic parenting.

With a steadfast dedication to the Islamic values of guidance, discipline, and affection, this book provides parents with useful tactics and methods rooted in Islamic teachings. Deep understandings and motivation are provided by the exquisite weaving of Hadith references and Quranic texts throughout each chapter. It provides a thorough parenting strategy that includes emotional intelligence, spirituality, education, faith, and media and technology usage in moderation.

This book will revitalise your spirit, fire your passion for parenting teens, and greatly impact the world, regardless of whether you're a fresh parent looking for direction or an experienced one wishing to improve your parenting skills. It is evidence of the life-changing impact of Islamic parenting, teaching you how to raise hearts that are firm in their pursuit of virtue, deeply attached to Allah (SWT), and compassionate towards others.

Let's dive in!

Chapter Two

Understanding Parenting in Islam

Importance of Parenting According to Islamic Teachings

The greatest gift a parent can give their children is a strong upbringing. However, with so many philosophies of effective parenting to choose from, it can be overwhelming and perplexing. It is impossible to overstate how crucial the house is to a child's development and how big of an influence it has on their personality.

A bad home environment in a child's formative years may hamper their growth. Parents' behaviours, responses, manners, and attitudes all have a lasting influence on their kids. Parents serve as an initial role model and mirror through which their children view their appearance.

Children today suffer from the ongoing neglect of their parents in terms of the upbringing they receive. They are dealing with a number of issues in their lives that their forefathers never encountered. It is the enormous responsibility of the parents of this generation to bring up the true and sincere inheritors of Islam. To protect the children from the oppression of the outside world, they must make every effort. Their primary responsibility is to raise them to the best of their abilities so that they can lead this Ummah and teach them how to live as Muslims in all spheres of life as they mature.

Children are undoubtedly greatly influenced by their parents, and as a result, they most often mimic their words and behaviours. Hence, it is the duty of parents to encourage their children's growth by creating a secure and engaging atmosphere at home. Parents must give their children a solid foundation and an accurate grasp of Islam in terms of its fundamental principles. In the Quran, Allah (SWT) commands parents to safeguard their families from the burning of hell in addition to themselves.

Allah (SWT) says: "O believers! Protect yourselves and your families from a Fire whose fuel is people and stones, overseen by formidable and severe angels, who never disobey whatever Allah (SWT) orders—always doing as commanded." (Quran 66:6)

From an Islamic standpoint, the fundamental source for guidance is the Quran and Hadith, which highlights the significance of nurturing virtuous, proficient, and respectful children. Islam considers parenting duty beyond providing for a child's physical needs; it also involves fostering their spiritual, moral, and intellectual growth. Parents must understand that it is their responsibility to see that they develop into industrious, fruitful, and, above all, godly people who will benefit the Ummah.

The Prophet Muhammad (PBUH) said: "When a man dies, his action discontinues from him except three things, namely, perpetual sadaqah (Sodaqatun Jaariyah), or the knowledge by which benefit is acquired, or a pious child who prays for him." (Sunan Abu Dawud)

Quranic verses and Hadiths emphasising the role of parents in upbringing

Islam views a parent's job as a combination of spirituality, love, and responsibility towards their offspring. Parents can help their children have a happy and religious future by teaching them the lessons found in the Quran and Hadiths. Let's examine Islamic teachings and the significance of Islamic customs in Muslim families' lives, emphasising how they help to raise a generation of moral and resilient people.

Islam clearly clarifies that Muslims must comprehend the value of being a parent, the necessity of preparing children for the afterlife, and the duty of shielding them from hellfire.

The Prophet (PBUH) said: "Each of you is a guardian and is responsible for his ward. The ruler is a guardian and the man is a guardian of the members of his household; and the woman is a guardian and is responsible for her husband's house and his offspring, and so each of you is a guardian and is responsible for his ward" (Sahih Bukhari)

This hadith places a strong emphasis on how crucial parenting is. More than only providing for and loving their children in this life, parents must concentrate on preparing them for the life to come. Parents will be held responsible for how they fulfilled this duty; to what extent did we as parents strive to uphold our children's rights and raise them to be law-abiding, educated, and contributing members of society?

We, as Muslim parents, would be failures if our children were constantly deviating from the path of righteousness and living immoral lives. Parents must grasp the basic ideas that hold their children accountable on the Day of Judgment—namely, that they are a test.

Allah (SWT) says: "And know that your properties and your children are but a trial and that Allah (SWT) has with Him a great reward." (Quran 8:28)

The verse above emphasises that the test aims to ascertain how parents will raise their offspring. Will they raise their children according to all Islamic values, which include kindness, love, and respect? Will they get them ready for paradise and the afterlife?

The fact that far too many people fail this test is regrettable. Muslim parents who neglect their children are missing out on an incredible chance for spiritual and everlasting benefits. Witnessing their children grow into obedient servants of Allah (SWT) is the most fulfilling and honourable experience for Muslim parents.

Children who are raised with strong Islamic values can continue to benefit their parents even after they have passed away. Through their prayers and good deeds, they add to the parents' record of righteous actions.

A parent who continues to receive benefits from their child's dua after passing away is truly blessed. This is the real prize that life has to offer.

Parents must realise that being a parent doesn't begin when the child is born. Islam goes far beyond this, teaching us to pray for pure and good children and to start all of our parenting endeavours with supplications to Allah (SWT).

"Our Lord, grant us from among our wives and offspring comfort to our eyes and make us an example for the righteous." (Quran 25:74)

"My Lord, grant me from Yourself a good offspring. Indeed, you are the Hearer of supplication" (Quran 3:38)

A mother's job begins when her prayer for a child is answered, and she prepares to welcome a new life. Throughout her pregnancy, it is important for her to recite as much of the Holy Quran as possible. Science has demonstrated that newborns can hear from the womb and respond positively to familiar sounds after birth.

This highlights the significance of nurturing the child early on. Once a child is born, one of the primary duties of parents is to guide their children in becoming a responsible and morally upright adult.

- **Giving a Name:** According to Islamic customs, one of the primary duties of parents is to give their child a good name.

- **Nursing:** A child has the right to be nursed by their parents. Specifically, nursing has a critical role in fortifying the relationships within the family, notably between the mother and her child.

Allah (SWT) says, "Mothers shall nurse their children for two complete years for any that wants to fulfil the period of nursing." (Quran 2:233)

- **Fair Treatment:** Treating children with fairness and equality is one of their fundamental rights. It is the parent's responsibility to treat all their children equally, without favouring any child over another based on gender or other factors. Unfair treatment causes children to resentful and hateful feelings they carry into adulthood. This also strains the relationship between children and parents. As the saying goes, treat your children fairly if you want them to respect you equally.

The Prophet (PBUH) makes explicit reference to this
right: "Fear Allah (SWT) and treat your children fairly"
(Sahih Bukhari & Muslim)

- **Providing Quality Education and Guidance:** Islamic education and training are crucial issues that must be addressed as they are one of the children's rights. Both men and women are obligated to acquire knowledge. Knowledge, particularly religious knowledge, is crucial for a child's development. It is especially vital to remind parents who may overlook the importance of Islamic learning. Parents must understand that caring for their children's physical, emotional, spiritual, and intellectual needs is their main responsibility.

- **Talking to Children:** Regular communication is the cornerstone of a parent-child dynamic; it significantly improves their bond. Children should always feel loved, supported, and encouraged by their parents. It's also critical to realise that parents should treat their children with kindness and friendship. For parents, gaining their children's trust should be their top priority. They have to find us so convenient that they eagerly anticipate our company.

- **Instilling Faith:** Developing Imaan and Taqwa in children's hearts is a great obligation and duty for parents. It takes a consistent approach to develop the religious spirit in them. Furthermore, keep in mind that parents are the ones who establish the basic framework of their children's personalities. To make their children faithful to Allah (SWT), parents must instil in them the true "faith, the oneness of Allah (SWT)". All of Allah's (SWT) rights must be taught to children. Parents should try to assist their children in learning the tenets of Tawheed. Given that these represent the limits of Islam, they should never be taken lightly. Beliefs influence actions, and children cannot be expected to seek to dedicate all of their energies towards pleasing Allah (SWT) unless they are taught to honestly submit to Him – with their souls, mouths, and actions. Their love for Allah (SWT) ought to outweigh their affection for anything or anybody else in this world. Islam is a religion of genuine belief and sincere faith, the foundation of inner contentment and real tranquillity.

As Allah (SWT) says in the Quran, "But those who believe are stronger in love for Allah (SWT)" (Quran 2:165)

• **Teaching Children about Other People's Rights:** From an Islamic perspective, it is crucial that Muslim children understand the rights of their Muslim brothers and sisters. This is especially crucial for those who grow up in non-Islamic environments. As a result, it is important to instil in children a sense of duty and respect for their parents and excellent relationships with their relatives and neighbours.

"Worship Allah (SWT) and join none with Him in worship, and do good to parents, kinsfolk, orphans, Al-Masakin (the poor), the neighbour who is near of kin, the neighbour who is a stranger, the companion by your side, the wayfarer (you meet), and those (slaves) whom your right hands possess. Verily, Allah (SWT) does not like such as are proud and boastful." (Quran 4:36)

Since children view their parents as their primary role models, parents must recognise that they set an example for their children. For this reason, parents must make a consistent effort to raise moral children. The idea that children see more than they hear is among the most crucial parenting guidelines. Therefore, parents must be aware that children pick up on their every move from an early age.

As a result, children will naturally attempt to emulate their parents if they witness them performing good deeds. Similarly, a youngster will emulate their parents if they witness them engaging in harmful behaviour. It is concerning that many parents are not carrying out their parental responsibilities in this area, often neglecting that their children are constantly watching them.

If we want our children to grow up practising their faith sincerely, it begins with the example we set for them.

Islamic perspective on nurturing children's faith and character

In Islam, raising children is a sacred duty that parents are entrusted with, one that calls for love, tolerance, and a strong dedication to fostering their mental, emotional, and spiritual development. Muslim parents must inculcate strong Islamic beliefs and principles in their children from an early age, especially in this world full of diversions and obstacles. Let's examine Islamic childrearing based on the teachings of the Quran and the Prophet Muhammad's (PBUH) Sunnah.

A child's path of religion is distinct and might change over time. These young people must contend with many distractions and uncertainties as young children in this day and age. By allowing your children the flexibility to grow in their religion at their own pace, you, as their parents or guardians, should be a patient, understanding, and helpful part of this journey. Children should be allowed to investigate their faith in a secure setting, and you should set an example of tolerance and understanding.

Early religious upbringing is a meaningful and fulfilling endeavour. It entails setting a good example, establishing a welcoming atmosphere, and encouraging candid communication. Children raised with faith, morals, and spirituality can better comprehend their role and have a solid moral compass.

Creating a Religious Foundation

Nurturing a child's faith in Allah (SWT), the Oneness of Allah (Tawheed), and their belief in Prophet Muhammad (PBUH) as Allah's (SWT) last messenger are the cornerstones of rearing an Islamic child.

Parents ought to set a good example for their children by being devoted to prayer, reciting the Quran, and comprehending and upholding Islamic teachings in their day-to-day activities. Children's ties to Islam are strengthened as they grow up in a welcoming Islamic environment at home and in the community.

Establishing a deep spiritual bond with Islam in children starts at an early age when they are exposed to acts of prayer. Parents are responsible for encouraging their children to engage in worship activities suitable for their age, such as offering charity, fasting during Ramadan, and Salah (prayer). Children are more likely to commit to their faith for the rest of their lives when worship is made enjoyable and meaningful for them.

For Muslims, the Quran is an enduring source of guidance that offers moral and ethical standards for living. Parents should teach their children the lessons of the Quran by having them recite it aloud regularly, explaining the meaning of the verses, thinking about what it means, and comprehending and following Prophet Muhammad's (PBUH) Sunnah. Teaching them about the lives of the prophets and the companions of Prophet Muhammad (PBUH), along with their teachings, promotes moral growth and deepens their grasp of Islamic principles.

Ultimately, setting a good example for your children is the most effective way to raise them in Islam. As a parent, you are your child's first role model, and your actions speak louder than words. By embodying Islamic principles in your own life and demonstrating sincerity, integrity, and piety, you inspire your children to follow your path and aim for excellence in all facets of life.

Character Development as a Priority

The fundamental component of Islamic upbringing is character development. Parents are responsible for instilling in their children values like patience, humility, kindness, compassion, and honesty. The Prophet Muhammad (PBUH) set an example for all believers by living these virtues. It is beneficial to inculcate noble values and behaviours in children's lives by encouraging them to follow in the footsteps of the Prophet (PBUH).

Prophet Muhammad (PBUH) said: "Every one of you is a guardian and is responsible for his charges. The ruler who has authority over people, is a guardian and is responsible for them. A man is a guardian of his family and is responsible for them. A woman is a guardian of her husband's house and children and is responsible for them. A slave is a guardian of his master's property and is responsible for it. So, all of you are guardians and are responsible for your charges." (Sahih Bukhari)

This hadith emphasises how parents are responsible for raising and directing their children in the direction of righteousness.

Challenges of Parenting in the Digital Age

It is difficult to be a parent and raise children, no matter what your religion or origin. Parenting philosophies and upbringing vary among parents, and each family determines these things in its own unique way. Regardless of where they reside or what kind of parenting works best for them, Muslim parents have a significant obligation to raise their children as Muslims despite the difficulties of parenting.

Recognising that the world we live in as parents is significantly different from our own is the largest obstacle. This holds true regardless of the nation you reside in, and it becomes even more complicated given the quick dismantling of barriers between cultures. However, you still have the task of motivating, encouraging, and instructing them. It's your task to get them ready for the world. Let's have a look at the principal worldwide shifts we encounter:

Impact of technology on parenting practices

Parenting in the digital age involves navigating the vast, unexplored areas of the internet and technologies in addition to the actual world. In a world where digital literacy is just as essential as reading and writing, parents face new problems in directing their children's development as screens become more and more commonplace in their lives.

Today's children are raised in a world where technology is an integral part of their surroundings rather than only an accessory. Children are being impacted by more and more digital factors in the modern digital era, such social media channels, which frequently results in the degradation of their time, nature, and creative abilities.

It's the duty of parents to ensure that their children not only engage with the digital age but also thrive while being safeguarded from any hazards given by this new environment; digital parents should also know what kind of parenting works best for their family.

Prophet Muhammad (PBUH) said: "Each of you is a shepherd, and each of you is responsible for his flock. The leader is a shepherd and is responsible for his subjects. A man is the shepherd of his family and is responsible for his flock..." (Sahih Bukhari)

This Hadith stresses the responsibility of parents. Unmonitored technology use can undermine this responsibility, allowing harmful influences to enter a child's life without the parents' awareness.

Technology can be very helpful for communication and education, but it can also cause youngsters to become dependent and distracted. It can be challenging to strike the correct balance between letting our children use technology for good and ensuring they don't become overly dependent. It is said that it matters how parents adjust to and react to the new realities of parenting.

The continual presence of gadgets and technological advances in their lives is one of the main problems of being a parent in the digital age. The urge to give children the newest toys and technology is another problem that many modern parents deal with. It can be tempting to give in to our children's expectations and constantly stay up to date with the newest trends in today's consumer-driven culture. But it's crucial to remember that material goods don't equal happiness and that real fulfilment comes from connections and experiences rather than tangible stuff.

Technology can become a distraction from religious duties, such as prayer (Salah), reading the Quran, or engaging in Islamic education. For parents and children, excessive use of technology may lead to a neglect of spiritual practices, weakening their connection to their faith and diminishing the time spent on activities that nurture Islamic values.

In the Quran, it is said: "O you, who have believed, let not your wealth and your children divert you from the remembrance of Allah (SWT). And whoever does that – then those are the losers." (Quran 63:9)

how can we overcome these obstacles and raise resilient, rounded children? Setting aside time for family time together is portant tactic. Rather than concentrating on material belongings, p an effort to cultivate enduring memories via shared activities ily outings, game evenings, and meaningful conversations.

It's also critical to establish limits on screen time and technology use. Encourage your children to play outside, participate in sports, and perform crafts and other offline activities. Reducing screen time can lessen children's sense of loneliness and dependence on technology while also aiding in developing critical social skills.

Schedule time for enjoyable and soothing activities, and don't be embarrassed to ask for assistance when you need it. In summary, raising happy, healthy children in the digital age is achievable with awareness, intentionality, and a solid support network. Parenting in the twenty-first century is not an easy undertaking.

Balancing Islamic values with modern parenting approaches

Keeping a strong Islamic identity is a challenge for many Muslim families in today's fast-paced, materialistic world. It's becoming increasingly difficult to raise children who stay rooted in their faith while juggling contemporary obligations like jobs and school. Let's explore how Muslim parents might address these issues and uphold Islamic principles and values.

As a parent, you should instil in your children the belief that living a life that aligns with Islamic principles is the true measure of success, rather than having financial money or social standing. By establishing this foundation, children are more likely to retain their Islamic identity, particularly in cultures that value materialism and independence.

It is particularly difficult to strike a balance between the Akhirah (the Hereafter) and the Dunya (this world). While giving their children opportunities for success and material comforts is crucial, many parents prioritise these over their children's Islamic education. This detachment can be especially harmful when children get older, and encounter demands from a culture that values individualism and secularism. Children may regard Islam as secondary, viewing it as a series of rules rather than a way of life if they are nurtured in a setting where monetary success is valued more highly than spiritual development.

The process of fostering and moulding a child's character in accordance with Islamic principles is known as Tarbiyah in Islam. A healthy Islamic society is built on the foundation of the family, and it is the responsibility of parents to make sure that their children learn about and practise Islam. Without the right Tarbiyah, children could grow up disengaged from their religion and think that material accomplishments are the only things that determine success instead of a person's relationship with Allah (SWT).

It is normal for parents to feel offended or enraged when their children start to turn away from Islam. But it's crucial to handle these circumstances with caution and discernment. Even while interacting with people who disapproved of the truth, the Prophet Muhammad (PBUH) was always kind.

Using harsh methods or severing connections with disobedient children frequently increases estrangement. Rather, parents ought to maintain an open channel of communication, showing their children that even if they disagree with every decision their children make, they still love and care about them. In addition to loving their children unconditionally, parents should gently remind them of their obligations as Muslims. They might finally be able to soften their children's hearts and convert them back to Islam by being compassionate and understanding.

It isn't easy to raise Muslim children in the modern world, but it is possible to help them develop a close relationship with their faith if you have the necessary perseverance, discernment, and dedication to Islamic principles. The secret is to put Allah (SWT) first in every area of family life.

May Allah (SWT) protect our children, lead all Muslim families, and assist us in creating a robust ummah based on Islamic values, Ameen.

Chapter Three

Parent-Child Relationship in Islam

Building a Strong Parent-Child Bond

Developing a close relationship with your child is a truly rewarding experience. It brings you joy as a parent and instils in your child a sense of confidence that will serve them well. Your relationship provides them with a sense of security, understanding, and support.

As both you and your child grow older and encounter life's challenges, this kind of link serves as the anchor that prevents them from straying from you and Islam.

The ultimate goal is to create cherished moments that will strengthen relationships. Below are a few elements that will support the early development of that bond.

Foundation of Love and Compassion

Islam emphasises that parents have a fundamental duty to provide their children with love, care, and basic needs. It is their duty to offer genuine love and safety while also attending to their children's spiritual, emotional, and physical requirements.

The Prophet once kissed his grandson Al-Hasan in front of a man who remarked, "I have ten children and have never kissed any of them." The Prophet replied, "Whoever does not show mercy will not be shown mercy" (Sahih Bukhari)

The most effective way to express love to children as parents is spending time with them. Whether it's games or actual sports, playing together is a terrific way to build relationships. Play enhances children's attention spans, interpersonal abilities, creativity, handling of emotions, and intellectual capacities. While having fun, they even learn how to accept defeat with grace. Engaging in play with your children also helps them view you as a supporter rather than someone who always gives them orders.

From a practical standpoint, it is crucial to ensure that your child genuinely enjoys playing rather than feeling it is something imposed on them. It's also crucial to pick the ideal time and location. As your child gets older, they might begin to explore shared activities, such as community service.

Aim for Ihsan

Ihsan strives for perfection in everything—worship, etiquette, academics, and worldly endeavours. As parents, try to practise being less judgmental, controlling, and overly protective of your children.

Encourage them to acknowledge and grow from their mistakes. Stress and honour, discipline, and hard effort over striving for perfection since Allah (SWT) made every child unique. Try not to compare your child to other children; instead, ensure they understand that you are merely encouraging them to reach their full potential out of a sense of duty and love.

Be Curious About Their Day

It's critical to organise events that encourage meaningful interaction among participants. Even though it's difficult given the busy routine of modern life, moments after prayer, family dinners together, and catch-ups before bedtime all encourage these kinds of conversations. Having tea or lunch in a cafe can also be a catch-up for older children.

The saying that families who pray together, dine together, laugh together, and stay together has some validity. Pay close attention, show appreciation for what's going on in their lives, and refrain from passing judgment or writing anything off as unimportant.

Islam encourages parents to empower their children to become independent and confident individuals. The parent-child relationship in Islam is one of mutual respect, understanding, and nurturing. By following Islamic teachings, parents can create a strong, loving bond with their children that fosters spiritual growth, emotional well-being, and righteous character.

Prophetic examples of nurturing relationships with children

In Islam, we have rights over our parents, and we also have rights over our children once we become parents. Children are God's priceless gifts to us, and as Muslims, we believe that human life is precious and that each and every child is an individual deserving of dignity and respect. Children should be able to grow up in a happy, healthy environment surrounded by love and appreciation. In God's eyes, every child is priceless, and they all need to be loved, cared for, and respected to reach their full potential.

Every Muslim parent has a divinely mandated duty to instil in their children a profound admiration, reverence, and affection for Allah (SWT), His Messenger, His religion, and the indisputable teachings within it. The upbringing of our successors is therefore of the utmost importance, and we must learn from the greatest human role model in history, the beloved Prophet (PBUH), who inspired many people not only with his words but also with his deeds, which serve as a source of guidance for humanity. The character of the Prophet (PBUH) was not limited to a particular time, region, nation, religion, or generation. Rather, he transcends time and serves as a timeless worldwide icon for everyone.

The Prophet (PBUH) said: "Indeed among the believers with the most complete faith is the one who is the best in conduct and the most kind to his family" (Tirmidhi)

Prophet Muhammad (PBUH) embodied the essential traits that all parents should aspire to possess. The Prophet's (PBUH) inherent mercy for all of Allah's (SWT) creations is undeniable. His kindness is unmatched, and he sets an example for all of us with the way he treats children—not just his own offspring. As a sign of his gentle love and mercy, the Prophet (PBUH) gave youngsters lots of kisses and embraces. Despite his busy schedule, he would also actively participate in their lives. For instance, once, he made a special effort to comfort Abu Umair (RA) at the death of his pet bird.

Anas bin Malik (RA) said: "The Holy Prophet (PBUH) used to come to visit us. I had a younger brother who was called Abu 'Umair by nickname (kunyah). He had a sparrow which he played with, but it died. So one day the Prophet (PBUH) came to see him and saw him grieving. He asked: 'What is the matter with him?' The people replied: 'His sparrow has died.' He (the Prophet PBUH) then said: 'Oh Abu 'Umair! What has happened to the little sparrow?'" (Sunah Abu Daud)

This hadith gives us an example of the Prophet (PBUH) going above and beyond to assist a small child, something that many adults would overlook as being unimportant. For the child, this type of interaction can foster open communication, trust, and validation.

The Prophet (PBUH) played with Hazrat Usama ibn Zaid (RA). When he was approximately seventeen, he gave Hazrat Usama ibn Zaid (RA) command of Medina's defence forces. How could he have been given so much responsibility at such a young age? Additionally, the Prophet (PBUH) urged his community not to discount Hazrat Usama's (RA) leadership because of his youth.

It was stated in a hadith that: "If you are criticising Usama's leadership, you have then criticised his father's leadership from before. By Allah (SWT), He was worthy of leadership and he was one of the dearest persons to me, and (now) he (Usama) is one of the dearests to me after him (Zaid)." (Sahih Bukhari)

Respecting children's skills and trusting them should not be a source of fear for parents. When you ask for a child's input and involve them in significant conversations, they will feel like a valuable family member, which can lead to building family bonds.

The Prophet (PBUH) advised to demonstrate great love for daughters as well; when Hazrat Fatimah (RA), the Prophet's youngest daughter, came to visit, he would always get up to greet her, take her by the hand, kiss her, and make her seat where he was. On the other hand, if he visited her, she would reciprocate. Despite their simplicity, these lovely deeds reveal their deep affection and regard for one another.

The mother of the believers, Hazrat Aishah (RA), re-marked: "I have not seen anyone who resembled the

Prophet (PBUH) in terms of conduct, way, and manners, more than Fatimah". (Aishah continued,) "When the Prophet (PBUH) saw her coming, he would stand up for her, took her hand, kissed her, and brought her to sit in his place. When the Prophet (PBUH) visited her, she would stand up for him, take his hand, kiss him and brought him to sit in her place." (Tirmidhi)

It's crucial to remember that respecting your child entails not just not disclosing their secrets to others but also not degrading them in public. As we've seen, Prophet Muhammad (PBUH) set an example for how to raise children. He has shown us how to show them how much we appreciate and love them for the blessing of being in our lives. It is our responsibility to understand the best ways to raise our children and apply these lessons to our daily lives.

Communicating love, respect, and empathy in parenting

Growing children mimic the actions of others quite well. They react similarly to others in the company of those who adore them and treat them with respect and empathy. It is our responsibility as parents to reassure our children that we will always be here to listen to them and that they are not alone. By "putting ourselves in their shoes," we achieve this. Their anxieties become our fears, and their feelings become our feelings. This approach lets our children know they're not alone and that we fully understand them, fostering empathy within them and creating a safe, secure, and trusting relationship.

Parental authority is upheld by showing empathy, love, and respect—not through giving in or giving up. In addition, children acquire critical emotional control abilities, and the bond between them and their parents is strengthened. It is our duty as parents to treat our children with respect so that they can learn the importance of self-respect and respect for others.

The goal of gentle parenting is to promote healthy behaviour and mental well-being in our children by developing a close, caring relationship with them. With gentle direction, empathy, and respect, parents can create a nurturing atmosphere that fosters healthy growth and improves the bond between parent and child. Children feel loved, understood, and respected when a stable attachment is developed through sympathetic and responsive interactions. By actively listening to them and validating their feelings, parents provide a safe space for children to express themselves and grow emotionally intelligent and resilient freely.

Effective Communication Skills for Parents

You communicate with your child through every interaction, and it goes beyond just your words. Your child picks up on the tone of your voice, the expression in your eyes, and the kisses and hugs you give.

Not only does your communication style help your child learn how to interact with others, but it also influences your child's emotional growth and future ability to form relationships. Effective communication with the children is the foundation of a solid, healthy family. Our capacity as parents to engage in deep conversation with our children influences their general well-being.

Effective communication is crucial in parenting since it establishes the basis for a solid parent-child bond. Children can feel safe and supported when their parents communicate well and foster an atmosphere of trust and understanding. Parents can better understand their children's needs by having honest and open interactions with them and actively listening to them.

Moreover, parents who communicate well can better set boundaries and expectations. By articulating their expectations clearly and concisely, parents may help their children learn what appropriate and inappropriate behaviour is.

This lessens the possibility of confrontations and encourages positive discipline. In general, having good communication with your children is essential to developing a close relationship. It enables you to influence your children's behaviour, comprehend their needs, and settle disputes positively and healthily.

By improving our communication abilities, we can establish a supportive atmosphere that inspires our children to express themselves freely, grow emotionally intelligent, and become resilient.

The methods and strategies covered below will give you useful tools to improve the communication dynamics in your family, regardless of whether you're a first-time parent or hoping to fortify your already strong parent-child relationship.

Let's examine the art of communicating with children, providing advice and doable tactics to help your family develop mutual respect, understanding, and trust.

Techniques for listening and understanding teenage perspectives

Listening to and understanding teenage perspectives is essential for building trust and improving communication between parents and their teens. Here are some effective techniques:

Active listening

Active listening goes beyond simply hearing your child's words; it involves paying attention to their thoughts and feelings. By engaging in active listening, you can improve your connection with your child and your communication skills. This practice shows your child that you genuinely want to know about their experiences and emotions, assisting you in becoming aware of what's happening in their lives.

Children who actively listen are more likely to feel heard and understood. You can demonstrate that you are interested in what your child is saying and that you genuinely care by making gestures like supportive smiles and confirming nods.

When your child speaks to you, getting to the same eye level as them can make them feel more secure and connected. Asking them "what," "why," and "how" enquiries demonstrates that you are paying close attention to what they have to say. This teaches your child how to tell a tale and what elements to add, which also helps them to become better communicators.

You don't need to speak too much when you are actively listening. The less you communicate, the more chances you have of comprehending what your youngster is saying.

Speaking with you helps your child's cognitive development as well. Your child will be able to think more clearly due to the opportunity to communicate their feelings and views without fear of rejection or judgement.

The Prophet (PBUH) would turn his whole body to speak to someone, not just his face. (Tirmidhi)

This hadith demonstrates the Prophet's (PBUH) attentive listening style, where he would give his full attention when communicating with others, setting an example of the importance of focusing completely when speaking to someone, such as your child.

Establish a context for free communication

Creating an atmosphere that welcomes candid conversation is crucial to communicating effectively with children. This entails establishing a secure environment where children may express themselves without worrying about criticism or unfavourable outcomes. Teenagers value their independence. Allow them some privacy while still being available to talk when ready.

Invest all of your attention in listening

Giving your child your undivided attention conveys the message that they are your top priority. It demonstrates to your child your availability and interest in their thoughts, feelings, and actions.

Be a conflict handler

At the same time, families naturally experience conflict, and a healthy and constructive resolution to a problem requires excellent communication. Parents should view disagreements as chances for learning and development rather than as fights to be won or lost.

Parents must set a good example for their children by using courteous language, maintaining composure, and avoiding placing blame or offering judgment. By doing this, they foster a calm and harmonious family dynamic and teach their children important life lessons about how to resolve disagreements in their relationships.

> *The Prophet (PBUH) said: "A good word is charity."*
> *(Sahih Bukhari)*

Encouraging good communication, including kind and attentive listening, reflects the charitable nature of good words and interactions. Active listening fosters positive dialogue and enhances relationships. By integrating active listening according to Islamic principles, parents can foster stronger, more compassionate communication with their children.

Creating an open and supportive family environment

Creating an open and supportive family environment for children, according to Islamic teachings, revolves around a balance between compassion, guidance, and instilling Islamic values. A child's emotional health is given priority in a loving family setting, which creates a haven where they feel loved, respected, and in control.

Because of this solid emotional foundation, they are better equipped to handle the rigours and demands of their life paths. Parents help their children acquire emotional stability by creating a supportive atmosphere.

Stress and anxiety are reduced in a caring environment where children feel appreciated and supported, giving them the confidence to pursue their goals in life. Here are some key principles:

Take part in family-friendly activities

Family bonding activities are essential to building a nurturing home atmosphere and improving relationships. For instance, organising recurring family get-togethers, game evenings, or potluck dinners offers chances for memorable moments spent together and fosters togetherness and connection.

Engaging in these kinds of bonding activities helps families strengthen their bonds on an emotional level and fosters a caring atmosphere where everyone feels respected and loved.

These family-friendly activities are encouraged in Islam, and Islamic teachings emphasise fostering love, unity, and cooperation within the family.

> *"And among His signs is this, that He created for you spouses from among yourselves, so that you may find tranquillity in them; and He has put love and mercy between your (hearts)."(Qur'an 30:21)*

This verse highlights the importance of love, mercy, and mutual respect within the family, which can be strengthened through bonding activities.

Creating a supportive environment

Creating a secure and caring atmosphere for children to learn, develop, and become emotionally resilient is an important part of maintaining a supportive environment. Open lines of communication, showing affection, and constant encouragement are all essential components in making children feel important and supported in the family.

Parents may foster a sense of identity and confidence critical to children's emotional development and well-being by carefully listening to their children's thoughts and feelings. In addition to promoting children's emotional development, this nurturing atmosphere gives them a sense of safety, love, and acceptance—all essential for their general happiness and well-being.

Use effective parenting techniques to build a helpful house

Positive parenting techniques are essential to providing a loving and encouraging home atmosphere that supports children's emotional development and well-being. Establishing unambiguous limits and offering emotional assistance are essential elements that foster a favourable family dynamic. For example, when parents set fair and consistent rules with appropriate punishments, children learn the value of responsibility and decency, which helps to create a safe and orderly environment at home.

Strong parent-child relationships can also be fostered by providing emotional support to children through listening to their worries, acknowledging their feelings, and offering consolation and direction. In the end, positive parenting techniques help create a caring and supportive home atmosphere where children grow, feel nurtured, and acquire the abilities they need to face obstacles in life head-on.

The Prophet Muhammad (PBUH) said: "The best of you are those who are best to their families, and I am the best among you to my family." (Sunah Ibn Majah)

Spend quality time together

Quality time is a priority for building enduring relationships and fostering a peaceful home environment. Spending quality time together improves family members' emotional connection, communication, and sense of trust, which promotes a caring and supportive family dynamic.

Organising routine family activities, like game evenings, vacations, or family dinners, offers chances for shared moments that strengthen emotional bonds and provide enduring memories.

By nurturing these values, an open and supportive family environment can be created, where children feel emotionally and spiritually enriched, growing into well-rounded, confident Muslims.

Chapter Four

Adolescence: Understanding Teenagers

Psychological & Emotional Development During Adolescence

O ne of the most important stages of life is adolescence. Adolescence, which is typically defined as the time between puberty and legal maturity, is a transitional age in both physical and mental development. It's also a period of many changes in schooling, training, jobs, and unemployment, as well as moving from one stage of life to another.

Puberty is a special stage of life that presents opportunities and obstacles to individuals. Teenagers are viewed as a critical stage in life that calls for intense parental support, empathy, and care.

Adolescence is the developmental stage between childhood and adulthood, a time of intensely expanding individuality. During this time, young people can be both admirable and challenging. Their bravery, persistence, insatiable curiosity about the world and themselves, and insistence on applying logic to connect their actions and feelings are commendable, as is their relentless questioning of nearly everything that comes into their field of vision.

However, this stage can also be challenging as their demands for answers and explanations can be equally persistent.

According to Islam, adolescence is one of the riskiest times in a person's life since it is a time of intense physical, mental, emotional, and sexual transformation, and it is also a time when the shaitan (devil) is eager to seduce a person.

Additionally, during adolescence, there is significant neural growth. Although not necessarily reliant on hormone fluctuations, this development is connected to them. Brain regions that play a role in development include the limbic system, which controls emotions, sleep patterns, and the desire for pleasure and reward processing.

The prefrontal cortex, which is in charge of the so-called executive functions—decision-making, planning, organisation, and impulse control—is undergoing modifications simultaneously. Adolescents experience prefrontal cortex alterations later than limbic system changes.

Psychosocial and emotional changes, as well as improvements in cognitive and intellectual capacities, are linked to changes in hormones and the nervous system. During the second decade of life, adolescents become stronger and more capable of abstract reasoning and rational judgment.

They also learn to think morally and logically. Adolescents' internal changes impact external changes; the differences between culture and society, such as social ideals and standards, as well as how roles, responsibilities, relationships, and lifelong expectations change, are examples of these external influences. According to Islamic teachings, for parents, understanding this stage of life of teenagers provides a balanced approach to nurture their development.

Understanding Teens' Transitional Experiences

Spiritual growth and development

Adolescence is a time for spiritual awakening. Teens may question their faith or feel distant from religious practices, but this is a natural part of their development. Islam encourages asking questions and seeking knowledge; teenagers should be encouraged to explore their faith deeply. Encouraging reflection through acts of worship, such as daily prayers, Quran recitation, and voluntary acts of kindness (Sadaqah), can also strengthen their connection to their faith during this crucial time.

Social changes

Identity: Adolescents are occupied with figuring out who they really are. Your teenager may exhibit signs of experimenting with new interests and subcultures. These are the years when friends, family, the media, and culture impact their decisions.

> *"O mankind, indeed We have created you from male and female and made you peoples and tribes that you may know one another. Indeed, the most noble of you in the sight of Allah (SWT) is the most righteous of you. Indeed, Allah (SWT) is Knowing and Acquainted." (Quran 49:13)*

This verse emphasises that true identity and nobility come from righteousness and piety, encouraging adolescents to seek their place in the world through virtuous actions rather than superficial affiliations.

Accountability: Your child might welcome increased responsibilities at home and school. This can entail serving on the school council and preparing dinner once a week. It may occasionally be necessary to support a shift towards more responsibility.

Self-reliance: It's likely your child will desire more autonomy over things like where they can go and how they can move around, who they spend time with, and what they spend their money on.

Your family's routines, connections, and your child's friendships will likely alter as your youngster grows more independent.

> *"Indeed, Allah (SWT) will not change the condition of a people until they change what is in themselves." (Quran 13:11)*

This verse encourages adolescents to take the initiative to improve themselves, fostering autonomy and self-reliance.

Principles: This is when your teenager begins to forge a more solid moral and ethical foundation. It'll be the time when they'll ask more questions. Your words and actions will shape their beliefs and what is morally right and wrong. For instance, speaking positively about women's rights will shape their perception on gender equality.

Fresh encounters: Your teenager will likely seek out new experiences, even if they include risk. This occurs when your youngster tests their limitations and capabilities. They must be able to express themselves uniquely as well.

However, due to how adolescent brains grow, your child may occasionally find it challenging to consider the dangers and implications of trying something new before taking it on.

> *"And do not pursue that of which you have no knowledge. Indeed, the hearing, the sight, and the heart—about all those [one] will be questioned." (Quran 17:36)*

This verse cautions youths to seek knowledge and be mindful of their actions when exploring new experiences, especially those involving risks.

Media: Social media and the internet can affect how your child learns about the world and interacts with peers. They pose certain risks in addition to their many advantages for your child's social development. The greatest approach to shielding your child from the dangers of social media and guaranteeing their online safety is to have conversations with them.

Emotional changes

Emotions and sentiments: Your teen may exhibit strong emotions and feelings, and their moods may appear erratic. They'll continue to learn how to regulate and express their emotions maturely, contributing to these emotional ups and downs.

> *The Prophet (PBUH) emphasised the importance of emotional control and patience. He said: "The strong man is not the one who can overpower others; rather, the strong man is the one who controls himself when he is angry." (Sahih Bukhari)*

Being aware of oneself: Teens' perception of their appearance frequently impacts their self-esteem. Your teenage son or daughter may experience self-consciousness regarding their appearance as they grow. They may also make physical comparisons between their body and that of their peers.

Sensitivity to other people: As they age, your child will become more adept at identifying and comprehending the feelings of others. However, even as they learn these abilities, they may occasionally misinterpret body language or facial expressions. As their parent, help them figure out how others are feeling.

The Prophet (PBUH) taught empathy and understanding others' emotions. He said: "None of you truly believes until he loves for his brother what he loves for himself." (Sahih Bukhari)

This encourages awareness of the feelings and needs of others, emphasising kindness and compassion.

Making decisions: There may be a phase in your child's development where they behave impulsively. At this time, it's important to remember that your child is still learning how to make decisions and that there are occasionally hazards involved with certain choices.

During this time, it might seem that you and your child are arguing more and more. This is typical of children who want greater autonomy. It's also a result of your child beginning to investigate opposing viewpoints and thinking more abstractly.

As children don't always realise how their words and deeds influence other people, they may accidentally offend you or someone else.

It may be helpful to know that early adolescence is often when conflict peaks, and these changes indicate that your child is growing into their own person. In the long term, your connection with your child will probably not suffer from these arguments.

However, you can get through this phase of your relationship by teaching your child how to resolve conflict and help them calm down.

Islam offers a holistic approach to nurturing adolescents into responsible, balanced adults. Supporting teenagers through this journey with patience, wisdom, and love ensures they emerge as confident individuals grounded in their faith.

Recognising Identity Exploration & Peer Pressure

One of the most significant challenges adolescents face is exploring their identity and the peer pressure around them. Let's take a further look at these aspects!

Identity exploration

When they reach adolescence, teenagers inherently start to doubt who they are. This period is particularly focused on identity development, which entails exploring important questions about their personality. The term "identity" has various connotations depending on the situation (e.g., gender, religion, national, professional, etc.). Hence, one primary concern of adolescence is identity development.

When teenagers transition from childhood to adulthood through inquiry and commitment, identity development takes place. If the shift is successful, identity integrates; if it is fraught with confusion, an identity crisis results. It is stated that teenagers' identity development is greatly influenced by their religious beliefs.

A key component of this identity formation is religion, which provides young people with a framework for understanding the world and their place in it.

The Islamic values of moral rectitude and religion accept and direct this phase of self-discovery. In this multicultural environment where other religions and other influences predominate, Muslim parents must make sure their children are raised with a strong Islamic identity.

As Allah (SWT) says in the Quran: "And I did not create the jinn and mankind except to worship Me." (Quran 51:56)

This verse reminds Muslim teenagers that life's ultimate purpose is worshipping Allah (SWT), which forms the core of their identity. As they explore who they are, it's the duty of Muslim parents to guide them to ground their self-understanding in their relationship with Allah (SWT).

If you start early, it's not as difficult as it would appear to help your child build a strong identity and individuality. To provide children with a well-rounded Islamic identity, parents need to integrate the many elements of religion, language, culture, and community. It's important to instil Islamic principles deeply in their hearts rather than just teaching them the fundamentals of the faith.

For children, having an Islamic identity means realising the importance of their religion and growing close to it. It entails educating children about the core tenets and practices of Islam, fostering values such as affection, empathy, and reverence in their hearts, and ensuring that they put what they have learnt into practice on a daily basis.

From an early age, every Muslim parent should inculcate the fundamental principles of Islam into their child's psyche. These characteristics characterise an individual as a Muslim. Among them are:

Belief in Allah (SWT): Assist your children in comprehending that Allah (SWT) is the One who created and sustains the universe.

Love and respect for the Holy Prophet (PBUH): Use the role model of Prophet Muhammad (PBUH) to inspire your children by teaching them about his life, teachings, and character.

Five pillars of Islam: Provide an age-appropriate explanation of Islam's core tenets. These include prayer, fasting, almsgiving, pilgrimage, and declarations of faith.

Children need to be exposed to the rich history of Islam as it's a way to help them develop a strong bond with their faith and culture. Encourage your child to engage in various activities that benefit the

Muslim community and bring them closer to its members. This will help them develop a feeling of support and a place of belonging.

Encouraging youngsters to comprehend Islamic principles and connect with the religion's rich history will enable them to develop into self-assured, devoted Muslims who uphold their faith and morals throughout life.

Impact of Peer Pressure

Another very common obstacle Muslim teenagers face is peer pressure when they seek acceptance and belonging within their social circles. People communicate, build communities, and form groupings anywhere in the world. Therefore, pressure to fit in with the standard exists wherever there are groups, no matter how big or small.

Islamic teachings provide Muslim parents with a strong framework to counteract the negative effects of their children's peer pressure by emphasising the importance of surrounding themselves with righteous companions. Motivating children to choose friends who encourage positive behaviours and adherence to Islamic principles can help teenagers resist the urge to conform to harmful influences.

> *The Prophet Muhammad (PBUH) emphasised the impact of friendships, saying: "A person is on the religion of his friend, so let one of you look at whom he befriends." (Tirmidhi)*

Supporting teenagers' spiritual growth & self-discovery

Your child's spiritual development is one of the most crucial growth aspects. Faith is the most important component of life. A relationship with the Creator is the foundation of hope and meaning in life. Our beliefs shield us from agnosticism, bigotry, hatred, and shallow materialism. Unquestionable value for every person, forgiveness, charity, and grace are manifestations of faith.

In Islam, spiritual growth is the process of getting to know Allah (SWT) better and making an effort to become more pious, devoted, and intimate with the Divine. It is about nourishing the soul, cleansing the heart, and directing one's actions and intentions by Islamic teachings and tenets.

According to Islamic beliefs, fostering children's well-being involves a full range of interventions and practices. Islam offers several strategies and techniques to achieve spiritual and religious well-being. These include knowing Allah (SWT) and all of His wonderful names and attributes, demonstrating how Allah (SWT) creates, maintains, and governs the universe and people, and teaching the fundamentals of religious doctrine to young people so they can eventually learn to follow their religious values.

Introducing and teaching children to behave in line with good values towards themselves, others, and their environment is essential in daily life. Most importantly, it involves instilling an attitude of soul, conscience, and pious mentality to foster moral education and cultivate an enduring and commendable personality. Presenting the stories of the prophets from the Holy Quran can inspire children to love and learn from their struggles to bring salvation to humanity, imparting valuable lessons along the way.

Important Aspects of Islamic Spiritual Development

- Maintaining a close relationship with Allah (SWT) by regularly offering the five daily prayers (Salah) and participating in other acts of devotion, such as reciting the Quran, pleading for pardon through repentance, and making dua (supplication).

- Highlighting and reaffirming the conviction that Allah (SWT) is one and that He is present and has complete authority over everything in life.

- Being aware of Allah's (SWT) presence and His commands are known as Taqwa. It requires a profound sense of humility and reverence, increasing self-control and morality by engaging in mindfulness and becoming aware of Allah's (SWT) presence.

"Verily, the most honourable of you with Allah (SWT) is that (believer) who has At-Taqwa. Verily, Allah (SWT) is All-Knowing, All-Aware." (Quran 49:13)

- Observing required Ramadan fasts which involves depriving oneself of food, liquids, and other necessities from sunrise to dusk to cultivate self-control and heighten spiritual awareness.

- Giving regularly to the poor and encouraging compassion in others by doing acts of kindness and charity (Zakat). The Quran has seventy mentions of zakat.

"The parable of those who spend their wealth in the way of Allah (SWT) is that of a grain of corn. It grows seven ears and each ear has a hundred grains. So Allah (SWT) increases manifold to whom He pleases" (Quran 2:261)

- Gaining a deeper understanding of Islam, one can study the Quran, the Hadith (the sayings and deeds of Prophet Muhammad PBUH), and the teachings of Islamic scholars.

- Attempting to abstain from immoral behaviour, if one commits a mistake, sincerely repenting and asking for forgiveness.

"And he who repents and does righteousness does indeed turn to Allah (SWT) with [accepted] repentance". (Quran 25:71)

This transformational ability sets Muslim children on a path of self-awareness and self-discovery through spiritual growth, learning more about their true selves and life's purpose. Early exposure to Islamic teachings is essential for a Muslim child's moral, ethical, and spiritual development.

This method includes teaching fundamental ideals drawn from the Quran and the Hadith, so they can lead fulfilling lives that are in accordance with Allah's (SWT) will. These teachings provide a thorough foundation for living a balanced and moral life, covering religion, worship, moral behaviour, relationships, and legal concepts.

By integrating these teachings into their children's early years, parents can guarantee that their children develop a profound comprehension and admiration of their Islamic roots.

Chapter Five

Parenting Styles in Islam

T he holistic paradigm of Islamic parenting is predicated on the rights and obligations of both parents and children. Islam sees parenting as a duty that is prescribed by God. It is the responsibility of parents to fulfil their guardianship obligations in front of God and their children. In Islam, parent-child relationships are governed by checks and balances. Children and parents have rights and obligations towards one another.

Let's explore different parenting approaches, how they affect adolescent growth, and how Islamic ideas of moderation and balance might be implemented.

This chapter also provides advice on how to modify parenting strategies to fit the distinct personalities of teenagers, making sure that their talents are developed and that behavioural problems are dealt with in a way that is both compassionate and firm.

Different Parenting Styles on Teenagers

The many tactics parents typically employ to raise their children are categorised under parenting styles. These parenting philosophies cover both the emotional milieu in which parents raise their children and their actions and attitudes.

Islam has imparted numerous lessons on good parenting practices that align with the Prophet Muhammad's (PBUH) life lessons. Islam actually sees parenting as a complete system that stems from parents' attitudes and behaviours towards young children in terms of properly nourishing, educating, fostering, acquainting, and leading them in accordance with Islamic teachings.

Parents utilise parenting styles as a pattern when teaching children. Giving and meeting their children's basic needs—such as those for food, drink, clothing, and other necessities—is only one aspect of parents' duty to them. However, it is more crucial to instil religious ideals in children at a young age since the religious instruction they receive now will have a lasting impact on their religious experiences as adults.

Within a family, parents are viewed as role models by their offspring, and as such, they receive great attention from them for everything they do, including imitating their parents' actions. Numerous verses and hadiths expound on the virtues of rearing children.

The Holy Prophet (PBUH) said that education is better than charity (sadaqah), He (PBUH) also said: "A person who educates his child (with a good education) is better than giving one sack (sadaqah)". Moreover, the Holy Prophet (PBUH) clearly reminded of the importance of family education: "the child is born in a state of Fitrah, and then his parents make him Jewish, Christian or Magian" (Sahih Muslim)

Authoritative vs. Authoritarian vs. Permissive Parenting

Let's explore different parenting styles, their impact on teenagers, and how Islamic principles can guide parents in balancing discipline with compassion.

Authoritarian Parenting

Parenting approaches that place a high priority on forming children's personalities often involve setting rigid expectations that must be met—typically with some warnings. This type of parenting is characterised by children who are docile and follow their parents' instructions closely. It features intense parental control over behaviour, one-way communication, and a strong parental presence.

Authoritarian parents constantly want to be in charge of their children, enforcing rigid standards without allowing for discussion or input regarding family decisions. As a result, youngsters are given instructions without any justification.

> *The Prophet Muhammad (PBUH) advised against such harshness: "Kindness is not to be found in anything but that it adds to its beauty, and it is not withdrawn from anything but it makes it defective." (Sahih Muslim)*

Authoritarian parenting can create a sense of fear and resentment in teenagers, leading to secretive behaviour and diminished trust. While rules and boundaries are necessary, they must be tempered with compassion, understanding, and respect for the child's autonomy.

> *Allah (SWT) advises parents to be gentle in correcting their children: "Invite to the way of your Lord with wisdom and good instruction, and argue with them in a way that is best." (Quran 16:125)*

Furthermore, authoritarian parents frequently attempt to create a wall between their children and the outside world. When this happens, children struggle against the severe rules that are imposed upon them. For this reason, even though we occasionally see the most devout mothers or fathers at the mosque, their children are never present. It's quite likely that parents' rigid rules discourage their children from performing religious duties.

Authoritative Parenting

The authoritative parenting style is the antithesis of the authoritarian parenting style. It is the best kind of parenting. Authoritative parenting, often known as democratic parenting, is a method of raising children that emphasises their sensible or reasonable interests to mould their personalities.

> *This approach aligns with the Islamic principle of balance, as Allah (SWT) says in the Quran: "Thus we have made you a justly balanced nation..." (Quran 2:143)*

This verse emphasises the importance of balance in all aspects of life, including parenting. Prophet Muhammad (PBUH) also exemplified this balance in his interactions with children, showing kindness, love, and mercy yet encouraging discipline and responsibility.

Some characteristics of this pattern include:

- giving children the chance to become independent and develop self-control

- recognising children as unique individuals and involving them in decision-making

- prioritising children's interests without holding back

- being realistic about children's abilities and not expecting too much

- taking a warm approach with the children

The chapter in the Quran, known as Surah Luqman, is a prime illustration of this parenting style. Hazrat Luqman (AS) gives his son important guidance for both this life and the next. In addition, he counsels his son on how to behave politely in public. Hazrat Luqman (AS) also lays the groundwork for his son's afterlife by praising prayer and patience and outlining the advantages of doing so.

> *"O my son, establish prayer, enjoin what is right, forbid what is wrong, and be patient over what befalls you. Indeed, [all] that is of the matters [requiring] determination." (Quran 31:17)*

This verse is part of Hazrat Luqman's (AS) wise counsel to his son, encouraging him to uphold spiritual and moral values and to show patience in life's trials.

Children raised with this parenting style exhibit behaviour, high levels of interest, self-assurance, friendliness, self-control, politeness, cooperation, and accomplishment orientation. When democratic and authoritative methods are used to care for children, this will result in a happy, creative, intelligent, resilient to stress, and well-liked child.

Permissive Parenting

Permissive parenting means giving a child very little monitoring and allowing them do things on their own. Parents who practise permissive parenting help mould their children's personalities. This parenting style is characterised by the freedom the children have to communicate their encouragement or desires, as well as the parents' near-complete abstinence from using punishment.

Parents who are lax in their parenting are typically too preoccupied with worldly pursuits and pay little attention to their children's mental and emotional growth. This prevents the development of the friendship that is so important in a child's life between parents and their offspring.

School is typically not a priority for kids who live with parents who are too indulgent. Furthermore, these kids typically receive material goods without ever having to work for them. Children raised in this manner are typically destined for failure both here on Earth and in the afterlife.

The parenting facets of this style are put into practice by the parents' lack of concern for their children's friendships, lack of attention to their needs, infrequent dialogue, particularly when it comes to complaints and requests for consideration, and lack of concern for the issues that their children face.

The Prophet Muhammad (PBUH) warned against allowing too much leniency. Parents are accountable for the upbringing of their children and must guide them with the necessary boundaries. Permissive parenting can create confusion in teenagers, as they may struggle with self-regulation and decision-making without clear guidelines.

Applying Islamic principles of balance and moderation in parenting

Islam teaches the concept of Wasatiyyah (moderation), which can be applied to parenting styles. Parenting in Islam is neither overly strict nor overly lenient. Instead, it calls for a balanced approach, where parents are firm yet compassionate, setting boundaries while nurturing a close and loving relationship with their children.

Ultimately, parents learn throughout their lifetime as a result of being parents. Parenting is not a one-size-fits-all game, and you may feel anxious trying to raise your children correctly but not understanding exactly what works. You will, insha'Allah, stay on course and feel at ease knowing that you are giving it your all and placing your faith in Allah (SWT) if you adhere to these fundamental guidelines. Most importantly, you must always offer up prayers for your kids, asking Allah (SWT) "Ar Rashid, the Guide", to lead them in the correct direction and assist you in choosing what's best for them.

Tailoring Parenting Approaches to Individual Teenage Personalities

Children's education for each Muslim parent is considered a big responsibility in Islam. The goal of every parent is to raise a generation of exceptional and morally upright people. Islam places a strong emphasis on appreciating the individuality of every child while implementing its values of moral upbringing, compassion, and guidance. Here are some key points that align with both Islamic teachings and contemporary parenting methods:

Recognising and nurturing unique strengths and talents

Every child has special qualities and strengths waiting to be identified and developed. It is our responsibility as parents to identify and develop these skills so that our kids can thrive and realise their full potential. We can assist our children in building a solid sense of self, boosting their confidence, and laying the groundwork for a successful and meaningful future by learning about their interests, paying attention to their innate tendencies, and offering the appropriate chances and support.

Early years are a crucial time for core learning and developmental milestones. Children's brains are exceptionally flexible throughout this period, allowing them to easily absorb new knowledge and adjust. Early identification and development of a child's special talents pave the way for future self-assurance, self-worth, and a passion for learning. As a result, this early attention can have a significant impact on a child's self-perception and sense of ability, which can affect not only their academic trajectory but also their general well-being.

The Quran reminds us of the diverse ways Allah (SWT) bestows His favours: "And [mention] when your Lord said to the angels, 'Indeed, I will make upon the earth a successive authority.' They said, 'Will You place upon it one who causes corruption therein and sheds blood, while we declare Your praise and sanctify You?' Allah (SWT) said, 'Indeed, I know that which you do not kn ow.'" (Quran 2:30)

This verse shows that Allah (SWT) has endowed each person with specific qualities for their unique role on Earth.

Finding your children's strengths and talents as parents requires paying close attention to their passions and areas of interest. Keep an eye out for activities that grab their interest and cause them to become excited. It might be anything from creating art, playing sports or showcasing a knack for critical thinking and problem-solving.

Foster their passions by offering chances for investigation and education in those domains. Give them a variety of experiences and freedom to try new things so that their innate abilities can come through.

Allah (SWT) mentions in the Quran: "And We have certainly honoured the children of Adam..." (Quran 17:70)

Every child is honoured with unique capabilities, and as Muslim parents, it is essential not to impose societal expectations but rather to embrace and support the interests that arise naturally in our children.

Nurturing your children's abilities and talents requires creating a supportive environment. Make sure they can express themselves without worrying about being judged or criticised. To grasp their objectives and desires, promote candid communication and attentive listening.

Engage in their hobbies and interests actively, demonstrating sincere enthusiasm and curiosity. Give them access to tools, materials, and resources that support their interests; this could be literature on their favourite topics, musical instruments, or painting supplies. Provide them the freedom to develop their skills confidently by fostering a loving environment.

The Prophet (PBUH) said: "Verily, Allah (SWT) loves that when anyone of you does something, he does it with perfection." (Al-Bayhaqi)

Muslims parents are advised to praise children's efforts, to teach them the value of hard work and persistence, reinforcing that their development is a continuous journey.

Finding a child's abilities and talents is just the first step; giving them the opportunity to develop their skills is essential to their development.

Put your children in after-school programs, workshops, or lessons based on their interests. Urge them to join groups or clubs so they can engage with peers who share their interests and advisors who can help them develop their skills even more. Seek mentorship programs, holiday camps, or community initiatives that provide specialised training or direction in their area of interest.

By giving them these chances, you not only aid in their skill development but also introduce them to fresh viewpoints and challenges.

As the Quran encourages: "And say, 'Do [as you will], for Allah (SWT) will see your deeds, and [so will] His Messenger and the believers...'" (Quran 9:105)

Celebrate your child's every accomplishment, no matter how tiny. As well as their achievements and efforts as they go through the talent development process. Furthermore, offer helpful criticism and direction to assist them in improving and getting past any obstacles they may encounter.

Finally, patience and understanding are essential. The Prophet (PBUH) exemplified this with his gentle and patient approach towards children.

He (PBUH) said: "Treat your children fairly and justly, and give them love and care." (Sahih Muslim)

By doing so, we fulfil our role as parents in helping them grow into their unique potential, equipped with faith, confidence, and the skills to serve Allah (SWT) and society. Finding and developing your kids' talents and strengths is a gift that can have a big impact on their lives.

Since each child is different, their skills may appear in many ways. Accept them for who they are, show them affection and encouragement, and watch them grow into self-assured, competent people who can have a positive influence.

Man has been declared the crown of creation and the earth's caliph by Allah (SWT), the Creator, above all others. This honour is primarily due to knowledge and wisdom.

The greatest leader of Islam, the Prophet Muhammad (PBUH), provided examples of essential ideas that can be used to cultivate positive values and strengthen character through knowledge and intelligence. It is available for consultation in several Seerah (lifestyle of Holy Prophet PBUH) literature for advice.

These tenets will help us educate society's members more effectively and comprehensively. As a result, we may raise our children to be better, more responsible members of society. These fundamental ideas were employed by our forefathers to educate society's members and enable them to live contented and peaceful lives. They changed them into responsible, valuable citizens in line with the teachings of the Quran and Sunnah.

We have learnt that the laws and guidelines found in Seerah texts are extremely important in helping children develop their personalities and characters. We should modify our parenting pattern in accordance with these golden rules to create a society that is thoughtful, kind, and forward-thinking.

The goal of our beloved Prophet's (PBUH) teachings is to provide every person with an equal chance for success and advancement.

"Wisdom is the lost property of the believer; wherever he finds it, he is most deserving of it" (Tirmidhi)

This hadith highlights the value of wisdom in Islam and encourages parents to seek and apply it in all aspects of effective parenting.

Addressing behaviour issues with compassion & discipline

Both blessings and tests from Allah (SWT) can come from having children. When kids reach adolescence, the test portion becomes clear. This results from a teen's quest for self and exposure to a wide range of viewpoints. However, sometimes this leads to behaviour issues in children, or, by nature, as humans, they tend to lean towards evil.

Children are inclined to engage in misconduct when they lack discipline. Since they lack the experience and maturity of adulthood, they are particularly susceptible to these impulses. It is more enjoyable and simpler to heed the guidance of the soul.

It takes a strong will to do what is morally and rationally correct. Although a youngster cannot naturally possess this, it can be acquired through discipline. Every child has the right to receive discipline from parents who are sensible and wise. To guide their child, a parent exercises control and discipline.

Islamic teachings state that as Muslim parents, we must start with the understanding that to achieve the desired behavioural changes in our children, we may also need to make certain adjustments to the overall hierarchy and structure of parenting. The balance between compassion and discipline reflects the comprehensive approach Islam advocates for raising children.

Children are Allah's (SWT) blessings, and they should be treated with love and kindness. The Prophet Muhammad (PBUH) was a living example of how to treat children with love and compassion, and he argued for providing them with equitable treatment and nurture.

Mercy and compassion are highly valued in Islam, and any kind of correction should never be applied with malice or violence. Parents are advised to consider alternative approaches to discipline that emphasise counselling and instruction over punishment.

As the greatest human role model in history, the beloved Prophet taught us, as Muslims, to place the utmost importance on raising our descendants. He inspired many people not only with his words, which provide guidance for humanity but also with his deeds, which serve as an example for others.

Prophet Muhammad (PBUH) also exemplified mercy in his treatment of children. He would play with them, show affection, and gently guide them without harshness.

The Prophet (PBUH) said: "He is not one of us who does not show mercy to our young ones and respect to our elders." (Tirmidhi)

Seek guidance on how to deal with misbehaviour in children from Prophet Muhammad (PBUH) as you traverse the highs and lows of parenthood. His actions educate us, as Islam does, how to raise children with kindness. Take a cue from his kind demeanour to raise your child with compassion and etiquette. Here are some tips to help you navigate:

Setting an Example: The Prophet (PBUH) demonstrated what he taught by deeds. Teach your child the right path by being kind to others and engaging in good deeds. Your behaviour teaches your child valuable lessons that resonate deeply with their heart and inspire them to imitate these deeds.

Compassion above Violence: The Prophet (PBUH) never used physical punishment when reprimanding. When cruelty was the norm, he decided to surround them with kindness. You too can use enjoyable techniques to gently guide your child towards positive behaviour, such as games and storytelling.

Timing is Everything: Part of being a wise parent is knowing when to offer advice. When giving advice, the Prophet (PBUH) understood the significance of the appropriate moment and mental state. You're more likely to receive an open mind and heart when you choose peaceful times to offer advice.

Keeping Your Attention in the Present: He advocated looking ahead rather than back. Assist your child in moving forward without the burden of past mistakes. Encourage them not to linger on them but accept the current situation as a chance for constructive development and education.

By following the Prophet's (PBUH) example, you're leading your child down a wise path. Your attempts to parent in a way that aligns with these prophetic teachings will shape your child's character; this is how Islam views character development.

Chapter Six

Digital Technology and Parental Guidance

In today's interconnected world, technology has permeated every aspect of our everyday existence. The digital world, with everything from smartphones to tablets, has many advantages but also brings special difficulties, especially for parents trying to parent children in this technologically advanced age.

There is no denying that children use technology a lot, and it has many advantages. It gives users access to knowledge and instructional materials that improve communication and accelerate learning. Teens can study, explore, and engage with the world in previously unheard-of ways, enhancing their social and intellectual development. Although there are many technological advantages, they also present certain difficulties that call for careful consideration in order to give our children a well-rounded and healthy upbringing.

In the midst of all of these difficulties, parents still have every day worries. Concerns regarding excessive screen time are widespread, with many parents sharing concerns about the possible effects it may have on their children's growth and welfare. These issues are exacerbated by social media demands, exposure to improper content, and cyberbullying, which negatively affects children's mental well-being and self-esteem.

The youth of today are undoubtedly being raised surrounded by media and technology. They have the entire world at their disposal, presenting amazing potential and challenging obstacles. Because of this, parenting in the digital era can be overwhelming.

Parents are concerned about their children's security, welfare, and health and about their own abilities to guide them through a complex digital world that is also new to them.

Relax! Not only is it feasible to establish a positive connection with technology and the media in your house, but it may also strengthen the bond between you and your child. Let's explore how to parent effectively in the digital age. After this chapter, you'll be equipped with the necessary abilities to raise your child's standard of living in the modern digital environment.

Challenges of Technology in Teenage Life

Children's interactions with the world around them have fundamentally changed due to the rapid growth of technology. A new generation of young people known as "digital teens" has emerged as a result of the digital age; these individuals are growing up in a world that is dominated by gadgets, online communities, and virtual experiences. But there are also a number of worries that have been raised by this digital revolution, especially with regard to the welfare of teens.

Islam emphasises that parents must be aware of the risks and repercussions associated with this digital age. Remember that technology is not inherently harmful. It is our duty as parents to provide our teenagers with the skills they need to improve their lives and to mentor them in doing so. With our help, they can get the best out of technology while avoiding its drawbacks.

There are no hard-and-fast guidelines for overcoming these digital obstacles, but as a Muslim parent, you can be sure that the more you support your kids in developing a stronger relationship with Allah (SWT), the fewer obstacles you will encounter.

Furthermore, we all recognise the transient nature of life on Earth. There's no disagreement on this. Everything in this life and the world, including feelings and attractions, is transient. Teaching your children to connect with Allah (SWT) is invaluable, as they may encounter additional obstacles as they become attached to others. Let's have a look at some of the key challenges they may face.

Risks and benefits of digital devices and social media

Humans are social animals with an inbuilt desire to interact and connect with others. In today's world, social networking has become the easiest and most appealing platform for connecting with others, leading to its attraction and subsequent addiction, especially among the youth who have shifted from physical socialising to the online realm.

As Muslims, the problem arises when the demand for engagement with the virtual world is met in ways that conflict with the boundaries set by our religion and culture. Because the virtual world obscures flaws and gives a false sense of independence and self-assurance, people tend to spend a lot of time—sometimes all day—on social media, which is troubling because it interferes with our connection with Allah (SWT).

The danger lies in how easily one click away can lead us, or our children, into places we purposefully never intended to go. This could result in dangerous encounters such as kidnappings, financial scams, or exposure to inappropriate content like nudity websites.

It's our responsibility as Muslim parents to monitor our children's and teenagers' internet usage, protecting them from harmful content, including pornographic and indecent websites. Maintaining appropriate protocols, together with strong accountability and oversight, is crucial.

According to Islamic teachings, digital devices and social media can have pros and cons for teens in the digital age. Using Islamic principles and values is important to ensure a balanced and responsible approach.

The Quran encourages the pursuit of knowledge that benefits. Allah (SWT) has stated: "Say, 'Are those who know equal to those who do not know?' Only they will remember [who are] people of understanding." (Quran 39:9)

As a Muslim parent, you have a duty to train your child to use technology correctly: to seek knowledge that enhances their education and helps them engage in productive activities rather than solely for entertainment. By studying the Quran and Hadith, you can find instructions on how to live a virtuous and guided life in all spheres, including communications and technology.

Risks of social media for teens

In Islam, social media mainly can present several risks for teens, as it can lead to behaviours and influences that go against Islamic values. Here are some key concerns:

Social media has developed into a powerful tool that many children nowadays use to express themselves freely, maximise opportunities for creativity, and share materials, papers, and other content and communication-related concerns with others.

It has encouraged pornography, public humiliation, bullying, spreading false information, creating false alarms, immoral acts and statements, wasting time, diverting attention from important and religious matters and deeds, and inciting violence in society.

Additionally, some publications and statements specifically disparage Islam and the Prophet Muhammad (PBUH), as well as obscenity, a rise in media violence, and invasions of privacy via social media. Thus, states, societies, faiths, and parents are seriously threatened by technological growth, particularly concerning social media.

This is because most religions, and Islam in particular, are under assault from the overt and covert harmful impacts of contemporary technology, which have a direct impact on children's and youth's moral and spiritual development and raise serious concerns about gambling, pornography, and other vices.

Excessive use of digital devices and social media can distract teens from their religious obligations, such as prayer (Salah), Quran recitation, and other forms of worship. Time management and setting boundaries are crucial in avoiding this pitfall.

Additionally, Muslim adolescents are often overconsuming social media. Because technology is so addictive, they frequently wind up on social media platforms for so long that they stop talking to their family in person, especially their parents. In this day and age, we see teenagers messaging someone on Instagram or TikTok who is sitting right next to them. Therefore, when social media usage increases and replaces in-person connections, it can negatively impact one's ability to communicate in real life.

One of social media's worst disadvantages is the abundance of meaningless rumours, frequently resulting in backbiting. In Islam, backbiting is considered a grave sin. Social media allows everyone a free and open forum to express themselves, yet many of the content that people share is pointless backbiting and slanderous remarks about other people.

As Muslims, we must steadfastly refrain from backbiting since it appeases the devil and enrages Allah (SWT). People might not be serious about this issue. But just as everyone will answer for whatever they do in their lives off the internet, they will all be held responsible for what they do online. Moreover, teens are at risk of being exposed to negative influences, including cyberbullying, peer pressure, and harmful ideologies that contradict Islamic teachings. It is essential to remain vigilant about online interactions and avoid harmful associations.

> *"O you who have believed, avoid much [negative] assumption. Indeed, some assumption is sin. And do not spy or backbite each other. Would one of you like to eat the flesh of his brother when dead? You would detest it. And fear Allah (SWT); indeed, Allah (SWT) is Accepting of repentance and Merciful." (Quran 49:12)*

> *The Prophet Muhammad (PBUH) said: "Do you know what is backbiting?" They (the Companions) said: "Allah (SWT) and His Messenger know best." Thereupon he (the Prophet) said: "Backbiting implies your talking about your brother in a manner which he does not like." It was said to him: "What if my brother is as I say?" He said: "If he is actually as you say, then that is backbiting; but if that is not in him, that is slandering." (Sahih Muslim)*

This hadith clarifies what constitutes backbiting and emphasises avoiding it, which is crucial for maintaining integrity in both offline and online interactions.

Social media is highly addictive. It might negatively impact a person's personal life if they become dependent on it. It could have a bad effect on a person's worship of Allah (SWT). It is possible to omit prayers, fail to fulfil religious obligations, or pray insufficiently focused.

Furthermore, excessive internet usage might be bad for one's health because it can prevent one from exercising. Moreover, procrastination and lethargy brought on by addiction can cause people to neglect their responsibilities to others, including jobs, education, and other commitments.

Children of Muslim parents realise the duty to ensure that their online persona accurately represents their religion by abiding by the Quran's teachings and the sayings of Prophet Muhammad (PBUH). Connecting with communities and like-minded people on social media can support one another in upholding modesty and abstaining from offensive information.

Muslims might further strengthen their adherence to Islamic principles by surrounding themselves with uplifting influences. To support the upkeep of a polite and safe online community, they can take an active role in reporting and flagging offensive content on social media sites. They can help spread the word about modesty and decency online by speaking out against offensive content.

Muslims may actively support modesty and avoid inappropriate content on the internet by using social media as a forum for spreading positivity, education, and ethical behaviour.

Benefits of Social Media

From an Islamic perspective, social media can offer several potential benefits for teens when used responsibly and in accordance with Islamic principles.

In the past, the only places to go for information about Islam were mosques, schools, and the wisdom of Islamic scholars. But in the twenty-first century, social media sites like Facebook, Twitter, and blogging have given Muslims a platform to research, ask questions, share knowledge, and connect.

Muslim youths can now interact with anyone around the globe because of these platforms, which have increased accessibility to Islamic scriptures and information for a broader audience. This direct interaction makes exchanging news, information, and discussions about Islam possible.

> *The Prophet Muhammad (PBUH) said, "Make things easy and do not make things difficult. Give glad tidings and do not repel people." (Sahih Bukhari)*

This hadith emphasises the importance of making things easy for others, being encouraging, and not being a source of hardship or discouragement, which can also be applied to how one interacts with family and others both online and offline.

Teens can study a variety of Islamic subjects in multiple languages, including the Quran, Hadith, and Islamic references. Online resources such as YouTube provide lectures and conversations about Islam in various languages, improving the quality of education. All things considered, social media is a useful instrument for spreading Islamic knowledge, encouraging discussion, and building a more knowledgeable and cohesive Muslim community worldwide.

Social media's capacity to facilitate connections with others that transcend geographical boundaries is one of the elements that drive positive usage of the platform. This also corresponds with Islam's goals. Teenagers can maintain familial ties using social media, which promotes solidarity and support among people who live far apart.

People can weave a digital tapestry of their lives by posting important life events, such as family gatherings or individual successes. This ongoing interaction strengthens emotional bonds, especially between distant family members, supporting the Islamic belief that strong family bonds should be maintained despite geographic distance.

Hence, social media offers several benefits for teens from an Islamic perspective when used responsibly. It provides access to Islamic knowledge, helping teens deepen their understanding of faith. Teens can promote good (dawah) by sharing positive messages and Quranic teachings. Social media fosters community among like-minded individuals, promoting Islamic values. It offers opportunities for charity (Sadaqah) and learning, aligning with Islam's emphasis on knowledge. By following Islamic role models, teens can gain valuable guidance. Overall, social media can be a platform for personal growth, charity, and Islamic etiquette.

Setting healthy boundaries for screen time and online activities

Concerns about the effects of screen time on our kids and how it aligns with our values plague us as Muslim parents. In addition, we can find it difficult to determine what constitutes suitable digital use for our children. Now, let's look at important aspects Muslim parents should consider if they wish to see their children using technology and screen time mindfully and intentionally.

Establishing limits is crucial to controlling your child's screen usage. To teach your child to live in moderation, think about designating particular times of the day when digital gadgets are permitted. Set guidelines based on Islamic teachings that emphasise moderation and mindful time use.

Alongside this, emphasise the importance of moderation, aligning time spent online with productive and beneficial activities. Encouraging them to replace screen usage with reading, playing outside, spending time with family and friends, and participating in other activities is equally crucial.

Being active and present in your child's digital life can assist you in understanding what they are exposed to and offering assistance when necessary. Creating a bond of trust and friendship will enable you to establish a more open communication channel with your child regarding their online activities and help you find common ground with them.

Islamic Guidelines for Using Technology Responsibly

Technology itself is neither good nor bad; its impact on our lives is determined by how we use it. Islam provides comprehensive guidance on how we should interact with the world, including the responsible use of technology.

Teaching digital etiquette and online safety from an Islamic perspective

It is important to teach children proper manners in the virtual world, just as in the real one. Let's discuss how to teach children appropriate behaviour when using digital networks.

Above all, and this should go without stating, make sure your children understand the importance of never sharing private information online. Tell them that personal information such as their home address, mobile number, bank account details, and so on should never be shared online or added to social media profiles. Additionally, let them know that it's better to communicate private information in person with family rather than online with random people.

> The Prophet Muhammad (PBUH) said, *"Whoever believes in Allah (SWT) and the Last Day, let him speak good or remain silent" (Sahih Muslim)*

This hadith teaches us the importance of speaking with respect and kindness, which can be extended to how we communicate in the digital world. Teenagers must be taught that the Islamic principles of modesty, honesty, and respect apply just as much online as in real life.

Respect and compassion are the two main tenets we should emphasise when educating children on digital etiquette. Let them know that the people they communicate with on the internet are actual people with thoughts and feelings, just like the people they encounter in person. Emphasise the value of being polite and respectful to everyone they connect with online, whether they are friends, classmates, or complete strangers.

Teach your children that interacting with strangers online is not a good idea, just as they wouldn't chat with total strangers in person. They do not need to reciprocate friend requests or follow requests from others. They do not need to interact with someone online if they don't know them in person or don't spend time with them offline.

As their parent, it is your responsibility to instil the value of making informed decisions regarding who they choose to talk to. Make it plain that people may more easily conceal their genuine identities and intents while online; therefore, blocking someone is perfectly acceptable if that's what they feel like doing.

Talk to your children about what cyberbullying is. Describe it and the potential harm it can do. Tell them that you or another trusted adult are available for them to talk to discuss their experiences, and motivate them to report every instance of cyberbullying they encounter.

Encourage your child to use social networking sites responsibly if they are old enough. Ensure that they are aware of privacy settings, the repercussions of excessive sharing, and the possible long-term effects of what they publish and say on the internet.

In summary, a critical aspect of preparing your children for life in the digital age is teaching them digital etiquette. By teaching them how to behave with compassion, respect, and responsibility in their online interactions will help them grow into responsible and polite digital citizens who can move through the online world with dignity and integrity.

Chapter Seven

Teaching Islamic Values in the Digital Age

Instilling Islamic Values and Ethics in Teenagers

I slamic principles offer a thorough foundation for moral behaviour, self-improvement, and social duty. Teach children these principles, and they will become morally upright, caring, and responsible.

These moral principles, drawn from the Quran and the Sunnah, support societal harmony, foster character development, and prepare them to be contributing members of society.

The moral and ethical precepts upheld by Islamic teachings in the Quran and Sunnah are known as Islamic morality and ethics. The Quran and Sunnah emphasise many of these moral and ethical values, including being trustworthy, patient, kind, humble, and polite. Teaching children these principles from a very young age is important.

The shift from adolescence to adulthood is a significant stage in a person's life, marked by a deep search for purpose and identity. Islamic values are important to teach children during this revolutionary time because they give them a strong moral and ethical basis that directs their actions, choices, and general growth.

The following are some major points that emphasise how important it is to teach Islamic values to children:

Moral Guidance: Islamic moral principles provide a clear moral code, defining what is right and wrong. Teaching these values helps youth understand the importance of kindness, compassion, honesty, and integrity in their relationships.

Coping and Resilience: Islamic principles strongly emphasise exercising patience, tenacity, and faith in the face of adversity. When these qualities are instilled in children, they are better prepared to confront life's challenges with resilience and an optimistic outlook.

Identity Formation and Sense of Belonging: As adolescents move from adolescence to adulthood, they must understand the core of their cultural and religious identities. Instilling Islamic principles in children creates a firm basis for their self-identity and a sense of belonging.

Decision-making: Islamic principles direct people to make moral decisions by considering the bigger picture and how it would affect them and others. The ethical framework becomes particularly significant when young people face problems in their personal and professional lives.

Long-Term Well-Being: In the end, teaching Islamic principles to children is crucial because it contributes to their long-term well-being.

These principles offer a comprehensive outlook on life, considering not just the material but also the social, ethical, and spiritual facets, all of which contribute to a happy and well-rounded life.

To sum up, instilling Islamic principles in children is crucial to raising morally pure, resilient, socially conscious, and capable adults who can make valuable contributions to their communities and society as a whole.

Islamic Ethics's Qualities

Islamic ethics is distinguished by a number of traits, such as:

Comprehensiveness: This encompasses every facet of human existence, including the social, political, economic, and personal.

Diversity: It has a variety of standards and ideals that are appropriate for every moment, location, and situation in life.

Genuineness: Islamic ethics are unique in originating from divine sources and representing the will of Allah (SWT). They are founded on religious texts deeply ingrained in Islam, including the Holy Quran and the Prophet Muhammad's (PBUH) Sunnah.

Comprehensive: They cover every facet of life and are filled with exact and comprehensive facts about proper human behaviour.

Accountability: Whether the accountability is individual or group-wide, it forces a person to take ownership of their words, deeds, and behaviours and refuses to make them reliant or place blame for their mistakes on others.

Procedure: It calls for the efficient application of moral principles and standards in daily life, as well as the performance of good deeds and true devotion.

Honesty: Islamic ethics forbid straying from the correct path and promote righteousness and perseverance in truth and justice.

Sacred: Islamic ethics derive from the Quran and Sunnah, independent of human influence. Consequently, survival, integrity, and health are associated with it.

Mercy: It calls for forgiveness and fosters compassion and empathy for others.

The following are important Islamic principles for teens:

- **Taqwa, or consciousness of God:** Helps teens arrive at choices with a sense of responsibility and mindfulness of God by fostering a consciousness of Allah (SWT) in all facets of life.

- **Sincerity:** Muslims refrain from lying, cheating, and deceit and value honesty in interpersonal relationships. Keeping one's word and honouring agreements, as well as speaking the truth even when it hurts oneself, are two examples of this.

- **Adab (Courtesy & Respect):** Emphasises the value of being courteous and respectful of peers, seniors, and other members of society, mirroring the Prophet Muhammad's (PBUH) teachings on manners.

- **Shukr (Appreciation):** Fosters a spirit of thankfulness by teaching children to recognise Allah (SWT) as the source of all their benefits and to be grateful for what they have.

- **Sabr (Patience):** Promotes resilience and the knowledge that hardships are a necessary part of life's journey by imparting the virtues of patience and persistence in the face of adversity.

- **Ikhlas (Sincerity):** Highlights the importance of acting with sincerity and integrity of intention, aiming to please Allah (SWT) rather than gaining attention from others.

- **Justice (Adl):** Promotes a dedication to equity and justice in interactions with others, regardless of racial, ethnic, or socioeconomic background.

- **Pardoning ('Afwa):** Promotes the act of forgiveness, enabling children to let go of resentment and develop empathy for people who may have harmed them.

- **Environmental Guarding:** Encourages careful environmental maintenance while recognising the Islamic duty to care for the planet.

Holding accountable (Mas'uliyyah): Emphasises accepting responsibility for one's actions, both as a person and as a member of a greater community. Educating children about these Islamic principles can help them develop into well-behaved, religiously grounded adults who can positively impact society.

Practical strategies for teaching morality, honesty and patience

Morality can be defined as a set of rules that guide us in distinguishing what is morally right or wrong. These rules direct us to act morally even when no one is around. Values, which can be exclusive to each family, are present everywhere. We instil qualities such as justice, honesty, integrity, kindness, acceptance, empathy, and respect in our children. Both our actions and inactions reflect our values.

Young children need boundaries set by their parents that they cannot cross. Establishing limits on morality and safety enables youth to make errors and learn from them. However, there are differences in how we draw boundaries between morality and safety. There is no such thing as total safety. We have to guarantee that our kids won't suffer any harm.

However, morality is something that cannot be imposed onto someone. We cultivate it as we help our young people think critically about their values and the possible repercussions of their actions. These are not lessons best learnt in adolescence. We start teaching them values as soon as they are toddlers. We should want our children to understand how their actions can impact others.

Hence, religion, society, the government, ethnic and cultural customs, and personal experiences are just a few of the many sources and experiences that teach children about morals and values. Above all, though, they learn from us as their parents and families.

Honesty in Islam and Arabic refers to not only telling the truth but also not defrauding others in life in general and business in particular. Therefore, in the context of business, honesty challenges the monopoly of commodities, the sale of tainted goods, and the sale of goods at a premium price. It's important to teach honesty to your child.

Allah (SWT) says in the Quran: "And the one who has brought the truth and those who embrace it—it is they who are the righteous. They will have whatever they desire with their Lord. That is the reward of the good-doers." (Quran 39:33)

Set your child a good example by never lying. Being truthful and honest will teach them the value of honesty. Avoid correcting your children when they tell the truth; instead, encourage them to do something constructive with their time and congratulate them for being honest.

"Righteousness is not that you turn your faces toward the east or the west, but [true] righteousness is in one who believes in Allah (SWT), the Last Day, the Angels, the Book, and the Prophets and gives his wealth, in spite of love for it, to relatives, orphans, the needy, the traveler, those who ask [for help], and for freeing slaves; [and who] establishes prayer and gives zakah; [those who] fulfill their promise when they promise; and [those who] are patient in poverty and hardship and during battle. Those are the ones who have been true, and it is those who are the righteous." (Quran 2:177)

Another Islamic moral trait appropriate for children is patience. It helps them tolerate life's slow pace and calm their impatience. It also helps kids get used to the idea that things won't always go as planned and might occasionally take an unexpected turn.

Prophet Muhammad (PBUH) said: "No one has been given a gift better and more comprehensive than patience." (Sahih Bukhari & Muslim)

The Prophet (PBUH) said: "Whoever remains patient, Allah (SWT) will make him patient. Nobody can be given a blessing better and greater than patience." (Sahih Bukhari)

Teaching your child patience is difficult as it involves teaching them to wait or sometimes politely denying their demands. While this may cause them to struggle at first, the long-term benefits will be well worth the trouble. It's important to remember to exercise patience yourself as you guide them through learning this essential life skill.

As Allah (SWT) says: "O you who have believed, seek help through patience and prayer. Indeed, Allah (SWT) is with the patient." (Quran 2:153)

Adolescents should be taught Islamic beliefs using a thorough and deliberate approach that fits their learning styles and developmental phases. Relevant lessons can be imparted through the use of captivating narratives, historical instances, and role models from Islamic history. Learning is made more enjoyable and meaningful by including interactive techniques like games and role-playing, and the principles being taught are reinforced through real-world examples like community service.

Open dialogue fosters critical thinking, and technology can boost engagement through instructional videos and applications. Children absorb these principles more readily when families are involved, creativity is encouraged, and lessons are connected to everyday experiences. Activities like prayer, introspection, and reading Islamic literature strengthen their spiritual ties. When the technique is adjusted to fit various growth stages, lessons are guaranteed to be memorable and long-lasting.

Integrating Faith-Based Teachings into Everyday Life

Integrating faith-based teachings into the everyday life of teens in Islam is crucial for building strong moral foundations and fostering spiritual growth. Early religious upbringing is a priceless and significant experience that can profoundly influence a child's moral and spiritual growth. Children should be taught an understanding of faith, spirituality, and fundamental life skills, morals, and etiquette. Here are some ways to do that:

Encouraging teens to perform their daily five times prayers (Salah) on time helps establish a routine that strengthens their connection to their faith. Salah, sometimes referred to as "Namaz," is the second pillar of Islam and is obligatory for every Muslim at the designated times. The act of offering Salah is primarily done to satisfy a duty, express devotion to Allah (SWT), and uphold religious observance.

Praying together as a family also reinforces the importance of community and strengthens the bond with Allah (SWT). As the Quran and Sunnah make clear repeatedly, Salah holds great significance and should not be disregarded.

Allah (SWT) says: "I am God, and there is no god but I, so serve me, and observe acts of prayer to remember Me." (Quran 20:14)

A Muslim boy or girl has an obligation to offer Salah when they reach adulthood. Nonetheless, parents frequently find it difficult to help their kids develop consistent Salah practices. Establishing this new habit could be challenging, but it is not unachievable. A few strategies for encouraging your child to consistently pray will be covered below.

Lead with action

Your children must witness you starting Salah with your own eyes before you expect them to start praying independently. One of the best ways to acquaint children with Salah is to demonstrate how to do Wudhu (Ablution) and allow them to observe you pray. Allow them to witness firsthand what you are promoting.

To inspire children to pray, we as adults must acknowledge that prayer is the most important thing we must do and should be our first priority. Children raised to value prayer above all else and who live their lives in prayer cannot be shaped by parents who find it challenging to pray consistently or do not prioritise it.

Understanding the Quran

Helping teens read and reflect on the Quran regularly is essential. Reciting the Quran is an integral component of our daily lives as Muslims. It is the word of Allah (SWT), and everyone who reads and considers it finds guidance, wisdom, consolation, and strength in it. As a result, we must teach our children to recite the Quran correctly and to enjoy it from an early age. Practice is essential to becoming proficient at reciting the Quran. Decide a time slot each day and stick to it! Practising even for a short while each day might have a significant impact.

Developing good character (Akhlaq)

One of the responsibilities Allah (SWT) has given to a believer in raising and instructing children is teaching Akhlaaq. Due to our multicultural society, it is becoming more challenging to instil in our children the value of good manners. Even if morality is universal among all civilisations, akhlaaq, or manners, can vary greatly.

We Muslims adhere to the teachings of the Quran and the Sunnah. We have a duty to teach teens the value of Islamic morals, such as honesty, kindness, patience, and humility. These values can be reinforced through real-life examples, stories of the Holy Prophet (PBUH) and his companions, and discussions on how these principles apply to the challenges teens face today.

Community engagement and charity (Sadaqah)

Involving teens in community service and charitable activities helps them understand the Islamic duty of helping others. Sadaqah, or charity and the giving spirit, is essential to Islam.

Sadaqah preaches selflessness and compassion while opposing greed and selfishness. From sharing their belongings with siblings and other relatives while they are young to nurturing them to be giving adults, we, as Muslim parents, have a duty to instil kindness in our children.

The Prophet (PBUH) stressed the importance of contributing regularly. As such, it is crucial that we instil in our children the idea of Sadaqah.

Allah (SWT) says: "And be steadfast in prayer; practice regular charity; and bow down your heads with those who bow down (in worship)." (Quran 2:43)

Fostering gratitude

Teaching teens to regularly express gratitude (Shukr) to Allah (SWT) for their blessings cultivates a positive mindset. In Islam, the concept of gratitude, or appreciation (Shukr), is very significant. It connects back to the fundamental reason we were created.

"And Allah (SWT) has extracted you from the wombs of your mothers not knowing a thing, and He made for you hearing and vision and intellect that perhaps you would be grateful (to Allah SWT)." (Quran 16:78)

As Muslim parents, you play a vital role in teaching your child how to express gratitude. Encourage them to recognise and understand that Allah (SWT) bestows upon us innumerable blessings, both great and tiny, every single day.

Children can better understand how fortunate they are when they learn to recognise these blessings. When your child adopts an "attitude of gratitude," they become better equipped to shift their perspective and maintain a more optimistic approach in the face of adversity.

This holistic approach ensures faith becomes a living, breathing part of their everyday actions, helping them navigate adolescence with purpose and integrity.

Chapter Eight

Balancing Secular Education with Islamic Identity

Challenges of Secular Education & Cultural Influences

Undoubtedly, one of the key elements determining a society's fate is its level of education. It is the primary instrument that helps form the character that young minds are developing. For the Muslim community, education entails moral and spiritual instruction that equips a person for everyday life and promotes societal advancement.

Islamic education is founded on moral upbringing, which uses admonition to bring religion and morals together. Compassion, integrity, truthfulness, humility, and justice are only a few of the great ideals regarding ethics and morals based on the Quran and the role model of the Prophet Muhammad (PBUH). In Islamic belief, a parent serves as a child's primary educator and is essential in instilling religious ideals in them from a young age.

During lessons, they use various techniques, including storytelling, exemplification, empathy, and altruistic dilemmas, to instil moral principles in their children and shape their morality and decision-making. Furthermore, Islamic educational institutions and community centres typically hold various workshops and activities to uphold young Muslims' morality and teach them appropriate behaviour.

The Islamic training system places a strong emphasis on moral and religious education, viewing them as intertwined rather than separate disciplines. At the same time, it embraces a comprehensive stance, recognising the equal importance of secular education and international knowledge.

Integrating Islamic and Secular Education for Holistic Development

In today's fast-paced world, it can be challenging for parents and kids to strike a balance between Islamic and secular education. Reaching this balance is essential for overall growth, ensuring not just academic success but also spiritual development. Here are some helpful tips and strategies to help you effectively manage both aspects of education.

First, establish distinct aims and objectives for Islamic and secular education. A balanced approach can be created by thoroughly understanding each's significance and how it contributes to overall development. Establish goals for spiritual development and academic success to direct your efforts.

To reinforce learning outside of scheduled study periods, integrate Islamic values and principles into daily activities. Recite passages from the Quran, observe Islamic principles in your everyday dealings, and participate in regular prayer (Salah). By this integration, Islamic education is maintained as a continuous aspect of life rather than a distinct endeavour.

A well-planned schedule is essential for striking a balance between education demands. Set aside specific time windows for studying Islam, secular subjects, and other pursuits. Make sure the timetable is reasonable and allows for rest and breaks. Maintaining a routine and sense of consistency helps support a healthy, productive existence.

Create a learning-supportive atmosphere at home. Promote candid conversations on academic subjects and Islamic principles. In addition to a peaceful, comfortable study area, ensure all required materials are available. Students are motivated in large part by parental support and involvement.

Use top-notch materials for Islamic and secular education. Use reliable textbooks, distance learning programs, and educational apps to improve learning. Sites such as Kulyat Ul Quran Online Academy provide extensive courses for Islamic studies suited to different skill levels and preferences.

Involve the community and educators to provide support and direction. Talk to educators about balancing education responsibilities while consulting Islamic scholars or regional religious authorities for guidance. Participating in community events or study groups might help you feel supported and a sense of belonging.

Instruct pupils on efficient time management techniques to assist them in juggling their obligations. Strategies like prioritising work, dividing study sessions into smaller parts, and utilising digital tools like planners can reduce stress and increase productivity.

Evaluate the success of your tactics regularly and adapt as necessary. Be adaptable and ready to change course when problems or situations arise. A balanced and rewarding educational experience can be maintained with the support of ongoing assessment and development.

Use engaging techniques! To make learning interesting, use educational games, multimedia materials, and group activities. This strategy can support motivation and interest maintenance, enhancing the effectiveness and enjoyment of the learning process. Balancing secular and Islamic education with careful preparation and commitment is possible. Equip yourself and your kids with the appropriate tools and techniques to improve your educational journey. Provide a comprehensive, rewarding educational experience by working together.

Supporting academic success while preserving Islamic values

As parents, we must understand that our children's lives are significantly impacted by their education. It opens their eyes to a world of incredible possibilities and enables them to explore interests and abilities they never knew they possessed. Education provides them with the abilities and information required to succeed in these and other fields, including science, art, business, and more.

Education is vital in Islam. Indeed, Muslims are exhorted to seek knowledge for the sake of Allah (SWT) in the very first verses of the Quran sent to the Prophet Muhammad (PBUH).

"Read! In the name of your Lord who created. Created man from clinging cells Read! And your Lord is the Most Generous he who taught by the pen, taught man what he did not know." (Quran 96:1-5)

The Prophet Muhammad (PBUH) also said, "Seeking knowledge is obligatory upon every Muslim." (Sunah Ibn Majah)

Managing faith and academic performance for Muslim teens requires a balanced approach integrating educational goals with strong religious and moral foundations. Encourage them to balance academics with religious duties by managing time for prayer, Quranic study, and school tasks. Introduce them to Islamic role models for inspiration. Incorporating Islamic studies into their education, fostering positive peer connections, and modelling resilience are crucial steps. Additionally, remind them to turn to Allah (SWT) through dua for guidance and success.

As a parent, the most important step you can take is to embed Islamic values within your home culture. This creates a solid moral foundation that helps teens remain connected to their faith while pursuing their studies.

How to Create a Faith-Centered Home Environment?

The environment in which a child is raised significantly impacts how their development into adulthood. A child's growth during the trajectory of approaching adulthood is influenced by various factors, including their daily routine at home, their social circle, and the activities they observe regularly.

The onus shifts to the parents/guardians to offer the child a constructive and healthy environment, as this will serve as the foundation for the child's future adult personality. By implementing the following strategies, Muslim parents can foster an Islamic environment at home and support their objectives for their children's character development.

Engage in at least one congregational prayer: Why does Allah (SWT) favour group prayer and advise His people to do so? Participation in congregational prayers is important for fostering a sense of community. Congregational offerings constitute a significant factor in strengthening the bond between kit and kin, fostering love and unity. The Friday prayers held at Ijtemah elevate the day's significance in the eyes of Allah (SWT), making it the most blessed day of the week compared to all others.

Make any spare space in your house into a dedicated prayer room where your entire family can congregate and say Salah five times a day. This will not only help establish a religious atmosphere but will also encourage your children to pray whenever they witness you saying a prayer. Together, your prayers will instil discipline and benefit the entire family.

Promote religious activities and worship: When children learn about Islam and its tenets through creative means, their interest in it grows organically. For instance, by donating Sadaqah, children can create and decorate their own Sadaqah box. It's best to introduce Sunnah practices to young children regarding this topic early on. Engaging in these straightforward yet fruitful rituals and prayers can enrich our lives, as they can be applied to everything from consuming food and drink to travelling.

Set aside time for deep learning: Choose a specific time when the whole family can sit together to study Islam. Sharing stories from the Quran about the prophets and the narratives of the Holy Prophet (PBUH) or his companions is especially beneficial when children are present. Every family member should be encouraged to learn from the story read each day and strive to improve and grow from those lessons.

Daily recitation of the Quran: The Quran provides a comprehensive guide to life that includes answers to all issues. It is a clear law that is revealed as the last, everlasting revelation to guide believers.

> *"This is the Book about which there is no doubt, guidance for those conscious of Allah (SWT)." (Quran 2:2)*

It is the parents' sole duty to instil in their children a deep connection to this holy story, which will act as a saviour for them on the Day of Reckoning when no one will be around to protect them from Allah's (SWT) anger and the fires of hell.

Observing the Sunnah daily: The Sunnah of our Prophet (PBUH) is incredibly straightforward and motivational. It includes straightforward prayers for every action, such as eating and travelling, and each

Sunnah brings blessings to our daily lives. Creating an environment that embraces these Sunnahs fosters a deeply Islamic atmosphere.

Align your family's lifestyle with your Islamic principles: As Muslim parents, try your hardest to live up to the lessons you are teaching your children. It is unrealistic to expect children to embrace a religious setting if the adults around them openly contradict Islamic principles. A positive Islamic atmosphere is built on the foundation of your behaviour, speech, and interactions reflecting your Deen.

As parents, you should sincerely fulfil your obligations to your children so that they may serve as a source of forgiveness for you in Akhira. This can be achieved by establishing and upholding an Islamically enriching environment at home. As Muslim parents, create an Islamic atmosphere in your home, keep a connection with Allah (SWT), demonstrate patience when facing hardship, and respect the rights of others, no matter how they treat you.

Your voice and counsel will finally be heard thanks to your thoughtful actions, creating a welcoming and Islamic atmosphere in your home.

Empowering Teenagers to Navigate Academic and Career Aspirations

For faith-based communities as a whole, abandoning one's religion is a serious offence. This is undoubtedly the case for Muslims, who hold that worshipping and believing in the one true Allah (SWT) is the primary source of our purpose and salvation. It makes sense that, as parents, our top priorities are taking care of and supporting our children.

This usually means attending to their requirements regarding their education (religious and secular) and their physical, emotional, and social welfare. As parents, we want our children to grow up to be responsible, self-assured adults who will embody their upbringing and make valuable contributions to society.

Parents' Involvement in Their Teens' Education

Parents can still play a significant part in their children's education even though most structured learning occurs inside school walls. Conversely, parents can inspire, drive, and even sway their children to succeed academically. New ideas, methods, and technology are continually reshaping how knowledge is taught and acquired in the educational setting.

Despite these changes, parents' role in their children's education is still vital and constant. The level of parental involvement has a significant impact on teens' academic performance, social development, and emotional well-being.

Let's explore parents' complex role in children's education, highlighting the value of proactive involvement, mutual aid, and teamwork between home and school.

As a Muslim parent, it's important you actively participate in your adolescent child's education, but you may need to explore several approaches.

High but achievable parental expectations increase adolescent success. In fact, these expectations are among the most significant factors that influence a 16-year-old student's achievements, credit accumulation, and likelihood of becoming a lifelong learner.

When children are exposed to high yet reasonable expectations, they learn to grasp and internalise the high value that their family sets on education. Regular support and conversations regarding school and further education also help students prepare for and aspire for university or training.

Parents can assist teenagers in being clear about what must occur to live the adult life of their dreams. As a parent, invite your teen to share specifics about their dreams. Enquiring "which university" or "what kind of job seems most interesting" might help them develop specific goals related to technical education, college, or professional options. Giving children something to strive for at this point is more crucial than selecting a particular job or career path.

Teaching your children time management skills is essential for several reasons. Parental supervision can help your child develop crucial life skills needed after high school and steer away from harmful behaviours. As a parent, encourage your child to participate in extracurricular activities, which can significantly impact their chances of getting into university. To help your child focus on their studies, limit their time spent on computers, video games, and TV. As children grow, the role of parents shifts from scheduling their activities to offering guidance and supervision. This is an equally significant duty!

Your involvement in your child's education during high school can be just as significant as in primary school. Parents can join advisory committees, site councils, and parent-teacher organisations just as they did when their children were younger. Parents may also be able to become activity coordinators, members of booster groups, and event committees.

Just to summarise, as a parent, you can significantly impact your teen's future success. Together, parents and schools can create a supportive environment that nurtures lifelong learning and personal growth. Moreover, empowering teenagers to navigate academic and career aspirations involves fostering self-awareness, goal-setting, and resilience.

Here's how you can support your teen in their journey:

Help them identify their strengths: Considering our qualities in a positive light is possible with a strengths profile. A group conversation about values, talents, and strengths in various spheres of life is the first step towards finishing a strengths profile. The personal traits that young people include in their profiles are their choice. Next, they rate each characteristic on a ten-point scale according to its importance, current state, and desired future state. Young individuals can pinpoint their areas of greatest strength and areas they would like to improve upon by comparing their scores.

Help them set SMART goals: Setting goals can lead to a fulfilling existence that isn't solely focused on material possessions. It's a skill that requires work. Objectives don't always have to be lofty aspirations. Yes, they must be SMART objectives. Setting goals might be intimidating. If carried out without a strategy or goal, it may result in disillusionment or desertion. Because SMART goals are so structured, they provide an answer to this. An acronym called "SMART" can be used to direct the goal-setting process. Objectives ought to be:

Specific: The objective should be sufficiently defined to allow teenagers to concentrate their efforts and clearly state the actions they want to take. It need not be overly broad.

Measurable: For progress to be tracked, the objective must be measurable.

Attainable: Although SMART goal setting is useful, it works best when the goal is doable. Your child is much more likely to succeed when they give themselves an attainable objective to work towards.

Realistic: The objective must be reasonable. Raising the bar will result in a fulfilling accomplishment. There must be some work involved.

Time-bound: The objective must be accomplished in a fair amount of time. Short-term objectives can be divided into manageable tasks that can be completed quickly. Over an extended duration, long-term objectives can be divided into time-based short-term objectives.

Teach them time management: One of the most precious resources is thought to be time, particularly in the modern world. It is commonly held that the key to achievement in life is the ability to skillfully handle this equal resource that we all possess. Calendars and planners will do more for your youngster than just improve time management. They are effective tools for managing workload and maintaining organisation.

Mastering the art of organising and prioritising, along with developing self-discipline, are increasingly important aspects of time management.

Have your teen make a schedule that balances homework, chores, and free time to help them learn important time management skills. Instead of hounding, establish explicit guidelines and penalties. Promote routines and offer time-management resources, such as calendars or applications. As you mentor them to learn from their mistakes, assist them in setting objectives, prioritising activities, modelling good habits, and setting limitations on devices.

Moreover, connect them with mentors for guidance and promote financial literacy to manage education costs. Encourage continuous learning and adaptability as they discover new passions. These strategies empower teenagers to make informed, confident choices about their academic and career paths while preparing them for future success.

Guiding Teens in Ethical Career Choices

The quest for wealth and success frequently takes precedence in today's fast-paced society, so Muslim parents must establish in their children the principles of ethics, accountability, and integrity—especially when making career choices. Following the guidelines of Halal (permissible) earning is crucial for Muslim families.

Not only does this guarantee your child's financial security, but it also instils in them a feeling of morality and responsibility. Muslim parents need to teach their teens about halal (permissible) and haram (forbidden) earnings. Islam has a strong focus on commercial dealings, particularly with regard to halal and haram.

Halal earnings are those acquired through permissible means, aligning with Islamic principles and ethics, such as honest work and fair transactions. Haram earnings, on the other hand, come from forbidden sources, such as fraud, interest (Riba), and illicit activities. Muslims are encouraged to seek livelihoods that comply with Shariah law to ensure both spiritual and material well-being. Earning through halal methods fosters trust and integrity and aligns with a higher moral standard.

> *Prophet Muhammad (PBUH) said: "Indeed, what is lawful is clear, and what is unlawful is clear, and between them are doubtful matters about which many people do not know. So whoever avoids doubtful matters, he has indeed absolved himself in regard to his religion and honour; but whoever falls into doubtful matters, he falls into what is unlawful." (Sahih Bukhari)*

The Quran contains Allah's (SWT) precise definition of what ha-lal (legitimate) and haram (illegitimate) means. Before deciding how to make money, one should consider Allah's (SWT) commandments about revenue. Islam has developed a scale to assess the validity of earnings and commercial profits. Says Allah (SWT) in the Quran:

> *"Do not devour one another's property wrongfully, nor throw it before the judges to devour a portion of other's property sinfully and knowingly." (Quran, 2:188)*

By incorporating these Islamic principles, teenagers can feel empowered to pursue their academic and career aspirations in a way that enhances both their worldly and spiritual growth.

Chapter Nine

Strengthening Family Dynamics

Promoting Family Unity and Harmony

A family is like a system, and every relationship inside the family is a part of that system. Any system component that is out of balance might cause discontent in the entire family. As a result, maintaining each of these connections is crucial to creating harmony within the family.

The Arabic word "usra" (family) derives its lexical meaning from terms that signify cohesion, intimacy, and safety. The word describes a collection of individuals bound together by strong bonds that preserve their unity.

Islam also values the family and views it as the foundation of society. Families are essential for raising morally upright people and pointing them toward righteousness. Let's examine the importance of family in Islam and how it contributes to strengthening ties and moral principles.

Islamic parenting encompasses family harmony in addition to individual relationships. In Islam, the family is seen as the fundamental unit of society, and it is everyone's duty to create a peaceful home atmosphere. A strong and cohesive Muslim family is created by spending quality time together, participating in acts of prayer as a family, and helping one another out when things get tough.

Parents' Role Towards Children

One of the most important components of Islamic teachings is the parent's role in the family. Allah (SWT) has outlined particular rights and duties for parents in the honourable Quran regarding the upbringing and nurture of their children.

It is, therefore, essential that parents comprehend and put these lessons into practice to promote a happy and healthy home life.

The Holy Quran, first and foremost, stresses the significance of providing children with a caring and loving environment.

> *Allah (SWT) says: "Do not worship except Allah (SWT), and to parents do good and to relatives, orphans, and the needy. And speak to people good [words] and establish prayer and give Zakah" (Quran 2:83)*

This verse underscores the duty parents have towards Allah (SWT) in raising their children respectfully and compassionately. Parents must provide a caring and nurturing atmosphere to foster their children's emotional and psychological well-being.

To provide their children with a sense of belonging and safety in the family, parents should interact with them with patience, understanding, and tenderness. In accordance with their resources and capacities, parents must make a concerted effort to meet their children's financial and educational demands.

The Value of Preserving Close Family Bonds

The Holy Quran emphasises the value of maintaining close family bonds. Family members should look out for one another, providing support and safety when needed. Sustaining familial connections guarantees a feeling of acceptance, individuality, and direction inside the family. It also fortifies our relationship with Allah (SWT).

Our families provide us with affection, assistance, and a feeling of community, which forms the cornerstone of our existence. Keeping close family ties is essential to the general well-being and enjoyment of every existence.

In today's fast-paced world, when time is limited and expectations are ever-changing, it is imperative to recognise the value of preserving and fostering these priceless relationships. This chapter covers the value of preserving family relationships among all of its members as well as the advantages of creating enduring attachments.

Keeping familial relationships intact aids in the development of a strong sense of belonging and identity, as an individual's history is shaped by family customs, values, and tales that are passed down through the generations.

Family relationships provide a psychological safety net during the highs and lows of life. Having a close family can provide comfort and peace in the face of hardships related to health, work, or any other extreme.

Family relationships are often the ones that we have with us for the longest duration of our lives. Together, the shared memories, loving gestures, and milestone celebrations create a tie that will last a lifetime. This makes it possible for us as individuals to communicate deeply, exchange money, and show our love and intimacy for one another.

A key idea stressed in the Quran is unconditional love for the family. The Quran emphasises the value of love, mercy, and compassion among family members. Fostering love and care within the family is one of Islam's core principles.

The Quran stresses the value of showing parents warmth and compassion by saying, "And your Lord has decreed that you not worship except Him, and to parents, good treatment." (Quran17:23-24)

Islam provides guidelines for family members' rights and obligations, guaranteeing that everyone is treated equally and respectfully. Husbands are expected to support their wives and children, and wives are expected to take care of the home and their families. Children must obey their parents and be grateful to them.

The honourable Quran emphasises the significance of family as a fundamental aspect of human existence. Families are crucial to the development of our personalities, moral fibre, and overall physical, mental, and spiritual health.

With love, support, and dedication, we can strengthen our family relationships and create a healthier and more purposeful life.

Practical Strategies For Fostering Family Harmony

When parents are unable to manage their homes effectively, there is little likelihood of harmony and peace inside the family. To foster harmony, parents must work together as a cohesive team, setting an example of cooperation and togetherness for their children.

If you put these tips into practice, you'll move closer towards creating a family that collaborates to build a happy, healthy home.

Pay attention to one another: Try to see things from your other family member's point of view. It's important to listen without planning your response. Rather, consider the reasons behind your child's or spouse's feelings. One of the best ways to demonstrate your concern for the other person is to listen to them. Active listening is one way to demonstrate to children—more than anything else—that they are valuable.

Talk to each other: A happy family must regularly contact all members. Hold weekly family get-togethers where everyone can speak honestly and freely without worrying about backlash. Discuss future plans and issues with your children, and give them explanations for any actions you take that they might find unjust. Your children are more likely to want to assist with any problems if you let them participate actively in family affairs.

Determine your family's mission: Together, develop a family vision that will encourage everyone to participate from the beginning as an active and willing member. Each family member must understand their role both individually and collectively within the family. This can also serve as a point of reference for resolving personal and family conflicts.

Create a trusting circle: Discuss how your method of communication as a family. For example, a family might establish guidelines for attentive listening, maintaining privacy, and being truthful. These principles support the development of a trusting environment that allows children to freely and honestly share with their family members.

Enjoy time as a family: Take the family on a day out at least once a month; it doesn't need to cost an arm and a leg. It could be visiting the zoo, a museum, or just going for a walk in the woods. Playing together as a family helps your children learn that teamwork also includes having fun. Keep in mind: a family that plays and works together stays together.

Prophetic Examples of Family Relationships and Solidarity

In addition to being a wonderful leader and Allah's (SWT) messenger, Prophet Muhammad (PUH) was a devoted spouse, a kind father, and a caring family guy.

His relationships with his family members provide us with priceless lessons about how to foster positive, harmonious relationships in our own homes. With the help of quotes from the Sunnah, let's examine certain aspects of his family life and consider the important lessons we may draw from it.

He (PBUH) said: "The best of you are the best to their families, and I am the best to my family." (Tirmidhi)

If a person doesn't show kindness to their family, Allah (SWT) will not consider them to be a fully committed believer. A sincere believer does not pick and choose based on personal preferences; rather, they follow the teachings of Prophet Muhammad (PBUH) in their entirety.

When Prophet Muhammad (PBUH) grew up, women had relatively limited rights. They were frequently regarded as property and considered inferior to men. Regretfully, the practice of burying live female infants was common. When he introduced Islam, Prophet Muhammad (PBUH) urged everyone to handle women with dignity and respect.

Prophet Muhammad's (PBUH) life story is replete with instances of the good deeds he performed for his family, especially for his wives. Hazrat Aisyah (RA) would receive his affectionate moniker "Humaira," which translates to "the red one," about her fair complexion when he would lie down on her lap.

To avoid upsetting his wives, Prophet Muhammad (PBUH) would also clean the house and wash his own clothes. The Prophet (PBUH) never spoke harshly to anybody. Even when he had to chastise his wives or children, he was incredibly compassionate with them. His treatment of his family is a glaring example of the principles he upheld. By following his gentle approach, we can learn to treat our own families with the same love, patience and gentleness.

Involving Teenagers in Family Responsibilities and Decision-Making

Involving your teenager in family responsibilities and decision-making can be a valuable way to empower them and strengthen family bonds, especially within the framework of Islamic teachings. Here's a guide on how this can be effectively implemented:

In Islam, the family is considered a unit to which everyone contributes. Assigning age-appropriate tasks to teenagers, such as helping with household chores or meal preparation, aligns with the Islamic principle of mutual support. This not only teaches responsibility but also helps them understand the value of hard work and teamwork.

Allowing teenagers to have a say in family decisions, such as planning family holidays, budgeting, or setting family goals, fosters a sense of ownership and respect. This involvement helps them develop critical thinking skills and a sense of accountability, as emphasised in the Hadith:

"The leader of a people is their servant." (Sahih Bukhari)

Incorporate lessons on financial management by involving them in budgeting for family events or managing their own expenses. This practical experience aligns with Islamic teachings on financial stewardship and accountability.

Engage them in community service or charity work as part of their family responsibilities. Islam places a strong emphasis on giving back to the community, and involving teenagers in such activities helps them develop empathy and a sense of social responsibility.

Create an environment where they feel comfortable sharing their thoughts and opinions. Regular family meetings or discussions can allow teenagers to voice their perspectives and contribute to family decisions, reinforcing the Islamic value of mutual consultation (Shura).

By involving teenagers in family responsibilities and decision-making and fostering strong sibling relationships, you can create a supportive and harmonious environment that aligns with Islamic values.

Chapter Ten

Parenting Challenges and Solutions

Common Parenting Challenges During Teenage Years

Although raising teenagers can be immensely fulfilling, it comes with its challenges. Adolescence is a time of fast change and development, both physically and mentally, and teens often face unique difficulties shaped by their personal experiences and backgrounds.

Nonetheless, parents can foster a supportive environment where teenagers can flourish if they have the necessary time, compassion, and optimism.

As they age, children never stop learning new things. They might encounter circumstances in their lives when you need to intervene and assist them.

At moments, you might feel like you're losing control or your cool, but that's completely normal. These situations frequently present a number of parenting issues that require care.

Common parenting challenges during the teenage years

Rebellion is a normal aspect of adolescence as teens begin to assert their independence and form their own identities. By challenging authority, they are learning to express their opinions and preferences as unique individuals apart from their parents.

Forming a sense of self, known as the independence of the adolescent personality, is a crucial part of being a teenager. However, parents may find it challenging to deal with their adolescent rebellious outbursts, particularly if their children and parents have divergent objectives, values, and views of one another.

Naturally, excessive disobedience can be detrimental to teenagers and their families. For this reason, it's critical to comprehend teenage rebellion and develop strategies for handling disobedient teenagers.

Having a rebellious teen makes parenting much more difficult, especially if you don't know how to handle it. Let's have a look at handling a disobedient adolescent while examining the reasons and, if required, potential remedies.

Setting explicit expectations, prioritising conflicts, employing positive reinforcement, and, if required, obtaining professional assistance are all crucial in dealing with adolescent rebellion. First, it is crucial to set realistic and unambiguous expectations for behaviour.

Establish a balanced approach by discussing both the benefits of good behaviour and the consequences of breaking the rules. By doing this, we help our kids learn and establish appropriate limits.

The Prophet Muhammad (PBUH) exemplified patience and understanding. Recognising that adolescence is a time of confusion and change can help parents approach their child with more empathy.

"And those who have believed and whose descendants followed them in faith – We will join with them their descendants, and We will not deprive them of [anything] of their deeds..." (Quran 52:21)

Positive reinforcement, which involves praising and supporting positive behaviour, works well. Teens are encouraged to behave well by celebrating their accomplishments and efforts, which also helps to create a happy atmosphere. It is vital to pick your conflicts carefully. Prioritise the things that really matter and learn to let go of small disagreements. It's important to choose your battles wisely since persistent conflict can intensify rebellion. Setting reasonable expectations and consequences is important in helping teenagers understand the significance of responsibility and respect.

"O you who have believed, protect yourselves and your families from a Fire whose fuel is people and stones..." (Quran 66:6)

This verse emphasises the duty of parents to guide their children away from harmful actions. If disobedience continues or gets worse, it may be wise to seek professional advice. Engage a family therapist or counsellor to address underlying problems and offer practical coping mechanisms to benefit the adolescent and the family. By using these techniques, carers and parents can deal with adolescent rebellion in a constructive way and seek to build a strong bond with their adolescent.

Sometimes, it can be difficult to communicate successfully with children, particularly as they become older and start to form their own opinions and ideas. It can be challenging for parents to communicate expectations, comprehend their child's feelings, and settle disputes. Strong, enduring relationships between children and their parents are based on effective communication.

Good communication fosters an environment of trust and openness in our kids, allowing them to express their ideas, emotions, and experiences without worrying about being judged or rejected. Through this open communication, children gain a sense of belonging and safety in the family, which also improves the parent-child bond.

Moreover, common issues include instilling faith and discipline and maintaining a balance between religious and worldly education. To address these, parents must lead by example by practising Islam sincerely, fostering a strong Islamic environment at home, and encouraging open dialogue about faith.

Discipline should be guided by patience, kindness, and understanding, avoiding harshness while emphasising moral lessons from the Quran and Sunnah. Balancing secular and Islamic knowledge ensures well-rounded growth and a deep connection with Allah (SWT).

Coping with stress and emotional turmoil as parents

Being a parent evokes strong feelings ranging from joy to hopelessness. Depending on the circumstances and the kind of support you have available, your sensations of love, pleasure, and pride could swiftly turn into feelings of hate, guilt, or rage. These emotions are entirely typical. Most parents occasionally feel bad about themselves.

To enjoy parenting and keep your house a secure and joyful place for your child, it's critical to learn how to control your emotions, including anger and impatience.

Controlling stress is essential to preventing its detrimental effects on behavioural and physical health. Anxiety, sadness, and other emotional health problems, as well as high blood pressure, can result from unmanaged stress. Discovering practical stress-reduction methods is an individual process. Although there isn't a single solution that works for everyone, the following useful advice might help you and your family:

Recognising stress signs: There are many different ways that stress can appear, and it's important to recognise these in both ourselves and other people; stress can cause you to lose your memory, become irritable, have trouble falling asleep, or overeat!

The Prophet Muhammad (PBUH) encouraged self-awareness and moderation in all aspects of life. He said, "Your body has a right over you, and your eyes have a right over you" (Sahih Bukhari)

Maintaining a journal might be useful in spotting stress patterns. It enables us to consider what sets off our worry and its effects on us. This activity is in line with the Quran's injunction to engage in introspection:

"And in the earth are signs for those who are certain, and within yourselves. Do you not see?" (Qur'an 51:20-21)

By becoming aware of what stresses us and how we respond to it, we may better understand ourselves and take action towards good stress management.

It is important to make time for leisure and happy activities, even when life seems too stressful. The Prophet (PBUH) stressed the value of spending time with loved ones and participating in activities that promote mental health.

Mental clarity can be preserved by taking short breaks during the day to engage in hobbies like reading, going for a stroll outdoors, or spending time with loved ones. Islam also promotes physical activity because it benefits the body and the intellect. Stress management requires maintaining both physical and mental well-being, which can be achieved through relaxation and health-conscious activities.

Islam refers to mindfulness as Tadhakkur (remembrance) and Tafakkur (reflection). By keeping us engaged and in the moment, these techniques help us break free from worries about the past or the future. The Prophet Muhammad (PBUH) frequently paused to think and ponder, particularly when he was in the Cave of Hira. By doing this, he was able to maintain his inner serenity despite obstacles outside.

Focus and anxiety reduction are two benefits of mindfulness. The Qur'an exhorts us to frequently recall Allah (SWT): "Verily, in the remembrance of Allah (SWT) do hearts find rest" (Quran 13:28)

Implementing other common but effective strategies—prioritising sleep, accepting emotions, supporting family needs, focusing on controllable actions, and building a support network—can help alleviate stress and foster resilience within ourselves and our families.

In Islam, stress is viewed as a test from Allah (SWT), and by approaching it with patience, reflection, and trust in His plan, we can navigate life's challenges with greater strength and tranquillity.

Islamic Solutions for Parenting Struggles

What parent doesn't think they have trouble raising their children? We all need parenting advice and ideas since, as we all know, being a parent is one of the most gratifying and difficult tasks.

Unless you've been given fantastic parenting advice, you undoubtedly ask yourself, "How can I raise my kids to be good Muslims?" Islamic parenting begins with parents setting an example. Lead by example, as the Prophet (PBUH) instructed.

There are a few parenting strategies that all parents should implement to create God-conscious children:

Seek guidance from religious scholars and mentors

Seeking guidance from religious scholars as parents can be a valuable way to integrate faith into your family life and decision-making. The first page of the Quran encourages us to worship and live in a close-knit community. We shouldn't assume that because of our limited knowledge, we have a spiritual mastery of what the Quran says.

Be careful not to succumb to hubris or complacency, as Shaitan would soon claim that we have mastered all wisdom and no longer need to study after touching the surface. A smart preventative measure is to have a scholar advise you in your routine endeavours.

Especially as parents, turning to scholars can deepen your understanding of religious teachings. This can help you nurture a home environment where values are aligned with faith and where your children can grow up learning from trusted sources.

To get the most out of seeking religious guidance, follow these steps:

First, identify your goals—whether for personal growth, spiritual insight, or resolving dilemmas. Knowing your objectives will help focus your discussions with scholars or mentors. Next, find the right mentors who align with your values and beliefs. They should be knowledgeable, approachable, and empathetic.

Prepare thoughtful, clear questions that relate to your specific concerns, ensuring more relevant guidance. Be open to learning and reflection, even when advice challenges your current perspectives. Regular consultations are key to ongoing growth, so schedule consistent check-ins to deepen your understanding.

Lastly, complement human guidance with prayer, seeking divine wisdom for clarity and reassurance. These efforts will make your spiritual journey more enriching and meaningful.

Parent with patience

One of the hardest jobs is being a parent. It takes a lot of effort, tolerance, and compassion. As Muslims, we look to our religion for direction in all areas of life, including raising children. Islam places great importance on forgiveness and patience, two traits that can support parents through the highs and lows of parenting.

Islam places great value on patience (Sabr). From an Islamic standpoint, patience is more than just waiting; it's about facing challenges with appreciation, faith, and tenacity. It's a means of achieving spiritual development and becoming closer to Allah (SWT). Parenting can be complicated, but patience is required when you and your child find yourself in a tough position where it's difficult to keep your cool and refrain from acting out or breaking the law.

Being patient is a crucial trait for any parent. Youngsters are inherently lively, inquisitive, and challenging to control. As they mature and expand, they push limitations and test boundaries. Parents must understand that such behaviours are typical and a necessary part of the process.

> *Islam views patience as a virtue with numerous benefits. Allah (SWT) says: "O you who have believed, seek help through patience and prayer. Indeed, Allah (SWT) is with the patient." (Quran 2:153)*

This passage reminds us that Allah (SWT) is always patient. When you see that you are becoming impatient with your child, take a step back, inhale deeply, and identify the source of your frustration. Talk about those problems instead of taking it out on them.

Be aware of what might cause you to lose your composure. When you were angry with your child in the past, what specifically incited your anger? Knowing your triggers will allow you to better employ coping mechanisms more effectively. There are several factors you can take to manage these triggers. Since Islam is a religion of peace, engaging in some of its spiritual practices, such as prayer, dhikr and reflection, can help you become more at ease, both physically and mentally.

Recite the Quran - *"And we send down of the Quran that which is healing and mercy for the believers, but it does not increase the wrongdoers except in loss." (Quran 17: 82)*

Make Dua - *"And your Lord said: Invoke Me, I will respond to your (invocation). Verily, those who scorn My worship, they will surely enter Hell in humiliation!" (Quran 40:60)*

Do Dhikr - *"Those who have believed and whose hearts find rest by the remembrance of Allah (SWT). Unquestionably, in the remembrance of Allah, hearts find rest." (Quran 13:28)*

Use empowering statements to remind your heart that you can do this, and don't hesitate to ask Allah (SWT) for support and direction. It takes a lot of tolerance and forgiveness to be a parent. In Islam, these attributes are highly prized to obtain Allah's (SWT) forgiveness and blessings. By exercising patience with our children during trying times and showing them forgiveness for their mistakes, we can foster an atmosphere that is full of love and understanding.

May Allah (SWT) lead each and every one of us as we navigate parenthood! Ameen.

Chapter Eleven

Nurturing Future Leaders: Raising Responsible Muslim Adults

Empowering Teenagers to Become Confident and Responsible Adults

The young people of today will be tomorrow's leaders and guiding lights. Thus, in order to be good parents, we must devote more of our time to raising our children so that they are more aware of their Islamic identity and develop into thoughtful, devout adults. As Muslim parents, we must work to develop our kids' resilience and self-assurance while also instilling in them the principles of Islam.

It might seem tricky to uphold these ideals in our fast-paced and demanding environment while ensuring our children are self-assured and autonomous. But don't worry, Islamic teachings can assist us. They are a comprehensive way to instil values, self-confidence, and responsibility in our young people, nurturing them to thrive both in this world and the hereafter.

Encouraging teenagers to have a personal relationship with Allah (SWT) is central to cultivating their confidence and accountability. As parents, we should teach our children the accurate 'Aqeedah of the oneness of Allah (SWT) and all necessary religious acts of worship to help them become closer to Allah (SWT).

The bounds of Islam are marked by the concepts of Tawheed, which is why they should never be taken lightly. Teaching the importance of remembrance of Allah (SWT) is considered the best way to remind Muslims of their purpose and responsibilities. When teenagers are grounded in their faith, they gain confidence from the knowledge that Allah (SWT) is always with them, guiding and supporting them through challenges.

Empowering Youth: Leadership Lessons from the Prophet Muhammad (PBUH)

Youth must develop leadership qualities since we live in a world that is changing quickly and becoming more interconnected. Leadership is a set of abilities, attitudes, and behaviours that enable people to have a good influence rather than merely being about roles or titles.

Adolescent leadership goes beyond conventional definitions. It involves exercising constructive influence over others, showing initiative, and choosing actions that will benefit both the individual and those around them. Leadership during adolescence also involves self-awareness, sensitivity, and adeptness in managing social relationships. In this sense, leadership is a collection of abilities all teenagers can acquire and apply. It's not a trait that is exclusive to a select few.

Given that today's youth will likely be tomorrow's leaders, it's common to emphasise the value of empowering and raising them. That being said, this idea is not new; leaders have always acknowledged the potential of the next generation. Prophet Muhammad (PBUH) was one such exceptional leader, and his interactions with the young people of his day offer a timeless example of empowerment.

Prophet Muhammad (PBUH) had a unique gift for connecting and communicating with young people. Instead of denouncing a young man for asking for forgiveness for a transgression, the Prophet (PBUH) handled the matter with compassion and counsel. Through contemplative conversation and spiritual guidance, the Prophet (PBUH) enabled the youth to make moral decisions and ask for forgiveness.

The Prophet's (PBUH) choice of Mus'ab ibn Umair as an Islamic ambassador to Yathrib (Madinah) is another example of how he empowered the youth. Mus'ab was entrusted, despite his youth, with the vital duty of disseminating the Islamic message in a society that was insatiably curious.

Because of his commitment and guidance, Islam was widely accepted in Medina, demonstrating the Prophet's (PBUH) faith in the ability of the younger generation to bring about constructive change.

By putting trust in young people, Prophet Muhammad (PBUH) showed that he believed in their potential. Hazrat Zaid ibn Thabit (RA) is a prominent example; at a young age, he visited the Prophet (PBUH) and expressed his desire to help with the community's defence. Hazrat Zaid (RA) was too young to fight, but the Prophet (PBUH) appreciated his intelligence and dedication to education.

Rather than rejecting him, the Prophet (PBUH) gave Hazrat Zaid (RA) academic responsibilities, which eventually led to his position as an official Quranic scribe and translator.

Hazrat Zaid (AS) was a great help during a crucial time when the Quran's preservation was in jeopardy. Hazrat Zaid (RA) was chosen by Hazrat Abu Bakr (RA), the first Caliph, to oversee the enormous undertaking of gathering the fragmented verses of the Quran into one volume, guaranteeing its preservation for future generations. This demonstrates the Prophet's (PBUH) vision of spotting and developing talent for the benefit of the community as a whole.

The Prophet Muhammad's (PBUH) philosophy of youth empowerment is timeless and will continue to inspire future generations. Let's follow the Prophet's (PBUH) lead by putting our youth first, giving them opportunities, and empowering them. They do, after all, contribute significantly to our success both now and in the future, making them more than just the leaders of tomorrow.

Encouraging active participation in community service

When a child reaches adolescence, the value of a group might become even more significant. Communities don't always revolve around a person's physical location, even though they can. Actually, there are two distinct meanings for the word "community."

A collection of people who live in the same area or who share a certain trait is referred to as a community. Another definition of community is "a feeling of togetherness with others, as a result of possessing common views, hobbies, and goals."

You and your teen can discover community in shared values, even though you can also get engaged in your local area. A community generally comprises individuals who value one another and have a sense of belonging. For early teens, a group can foster a sense of community, support from one another, increased influence, and exploration.

Encouraging teens to participate in community service is a way for parents to nurture empathy and a sense of responsibility. Islam emphasises the importance of helping others. This below hadith underscores the value of community service in fulfilling our duties towards society.

Parents can lead by example, as the Prophet Muhammad (PBUH) said: "The best of people are those that bring most benefit to the rest of mankind." (Daraqutni, Hasan)

When teens witness their parents serving others, they are more likely to follow. It is also important to connect service with their interests, making it enjoyable and meaningful for them. Parents should emphasise the rewards of serving others, both in this life and the hereafter.

As the Prophet (PBUH) said, "He who relieves the hardship of a believer in this world, Allah (SWT) will relieve his hardship on the Day of Judgment" (Sahih Muslim)

Encourage participation without pressure, letting teens choose projects that inspire them. Afterwards, reflect on their experience to instil gratitude and further their motivation. Through these efforts, parents can instil in their teens the importance of contributing positively to their communities.

Inspiring Teenagers to Embody Islamic Values in their Lives

Islamic teachings offer a rich reservoir of knowledge and direction for raising children that cuts beyond age and space. As Muslim parents, we aim to raise our children to be kind, polite, and morally pure people who live out the richness and beauty of Islamic teachings by instilling these timeless values at a young age.

Early training is crucial for instilling Islamic ideals in children. Studies have indicated that young infants respond more to new knowledge and moral principles. In addition, the formative years are crucial for forming a child's values and worldview.

Children with a solid Islamic moral basis in these early years are more likely to internalise and carry these principles into maturity. Let's review the key Islamic principles and discuss useful methods and techniques for instilling them in young people.

Recognising Islamic Principles

The tenets and convictions of Islam serve as guidance for Muslims' conduct. They come from three sources: the Quran, the Hadith (the sayings and deeds of the Prophet Muhammad PBUH), and the Sunnah (the Prophet Muhammad's PBUH style of life).

Among the most significant Islamic principles are:

Taqwa (Piety and Fear of God)

Taqwa refers to the consciousness and fear of Allah (SWT), driving believers to live righteously and avoid actions displeasing to God. It is often described as a protective shield that keeps people mindful of their responsibilities towards Allah (SWT).

> *The Prophet Muhammad (PBUH) said: "Fear Allah (SWT) wherever you are and follow up a bad deed with a good one, which will wipe it out, and behave well towards people." (Tirmidhi)*

> *"O you who believe! Fear Allah (SWT) as He should be feared, and do not die except as Muslims [in submission to Him]." (Quran 3:102)*

Ihsan (Excellence in Worship and Good Deeds)

Ihsan is the highest level of faith, where one worships Allah (SWT) as if they can see Him, or, though they cannot see Him, they are aware that He sees them. This level of spiritual excellence extends beyond acts of worship to every deed, inspiring believers to do well with sincerity.

"Indeed, Allah (SWT) commands justice and Ihsan (excellence) and giving to relatives and forbids immorality and bad conduct and oppression." (Quran 16:90)

"It is to worship Allah (SWT) as though you see Him, and though you do not see Him, know that He sees you." (Sahih Muslim)

Trustworthiness

Trustworthiness is a key characteristic of a believer, manifesting in honesty, dependability, and fulfilling responsibilities. The Prophet Muhammad (PBUH) was known as "Al-Amin" (The Trustworthy), highlighting the importance of trust in Islam.

"Indeed, Allah (SWT) commands you to render trusts to whom they are due..." (Quran 4:58)

The Prophet (PBUH) said: "The one who does not fulfil the trust has no faith, and the one who does not keep promises has no religion." (Ahmad)

Trustworthiness is the foundation of social justice and harmony, and betraying trust is seen as a sign of hypocrisy in Islam.

Honesty

Honesty, or Sidq, is a fundamental virtue in Islam. Being truthful in words, actions, and intentions is emphasised repeatedly in the Quran and hadith.

"O you who have believed, fear Allah (SWT) and be with those who are true." (Quran 9:119)

The Prophet Muhammad (PBUH) said: "Truthfulness leads to righteousness, and righteousness leads to Paradise." (Sahih Bukhari)

Kindness

Islam encourages kindness towards all of Allah's (SWT) creation. This includes kindness to humans, animals, and even the environment. Kindness is considered a means of attaining Allah's (SWT) mercy.

"Indeed, Allah (SWT) is with those who fear Him and those who are doers of good." (Quran 16:128)

Generosity

Generosity is highly encouraged in Islam. It goes beyond financial charity and includes being generous with time and kindness to others.

"The example of those who spend their wealth in the way of Allah (SWT) is like a seed of grain that sprouts seven ears; in every ear, there are a hundred grains." (Quran 2:261)

The Prophet (PBUH) said: "The believer's shade on the Day of Resurrection will be his charity." (Tirmidhi)

Generosity is a way to purify wealth and the soul and a source of reward in this life and the hereafter.

Integrating Islamic ideals into routine activities is one of the best methods to impart these values to kids. Parents can teach their kids to say their prayers, donate to charities, and treat people with kindness and respect. When ingrained in children's everyday routines, these behaviours become automatic and are more likely to be internalised.

Giving kids good role models who live up to Islamic principles can make a big difference in their development. Youngsters are more likely to absorb and incorporate Islamic principles into their lives if they witness others adhering to and practising them.

Parents, teachers, spiritual figures, and other community members can all serve as positive role models. Role models who exemplify these qualities can help children comprehend the significance of these principles and how to apply them in practical scenarios.

Chapter Twelve

Conclusion

P arenting teenagers in today's fast-paced, digital world is a journey filled with both challenges and opportunities. As we navigate the complexities of modern life, it's essential to remember the timeless wisdom of our faith. Allah (SWT) has entrusted us with the responsibility of guiding and nurturing our children, reminding us in the Quran,

> *"And those who say, 'Our Lord, grant us from among our wives and offspring comfort to our eyes and make us an example for the righteous.'" (Qur'an 25:74)*

This verse serves as a profound reminder of the importance of fostering strong, faith-centered families that can serve as beacons of righteousness in the world.

Throughout this book, we have explored how Islamic principles can be applied to the everyday realities of parenting in the 21st century.

From understanding the psychological and emotional development of teenagers to addressing the challenges of technology and secular influences, we have sought to provide practical solutions grounded in the Quran and Sunnah. By instilling Islamic values, fostering open communication, and setting a positive example, we can inspire our teenagers to become responsible, confident adults who embody the teachings of Islam in their personal and professional lives.

As parents, we must continue to guide our children with compassion, wisdom, and faith. The trials they face today, from the influences of social media to the pressures of secular education, require us to be ever-present, adaptable, and supportive. But above all, we must place our trust in Allah (SWT), knowing that He is the ultimate guide and protector of our families.

May Allah (SWT) grant us the strength, patience, and wisdom to raise our children with faith and integrity, helping them become the future leaders of the Ummah. May He bless our efforts and guide our teenagers to embody the best Islamic values in all they do. Ameen.

Find Out More

Website: www.barakahinbusiness.com

Socials: @barakahinbusiness

If you enjoyed this book, kindly leave a review to help expand our reach so others may benefit also.

Milton Keynes UK
Ingram Content Group UK Ltd.
UKHW021925281024
450365UK00017B/964

9 798227 208422